Chick Flicks

GROUP'S
DINNER
A AND **MOVIE**

Friendship, Faith, and Fun for **Women's Groups**

Group

Loveland, Colorado

www.group.com

Group resources actually work!

This Group resource helps you focus on **"The 1 Thing®"**— a life-changing relationship with Jesus Christ. "The 1 Thing" incorporates our **R.E.A.L.** approach to ministry. It reinforces a growing friendship with Jesus, encourages long-term learning, and results in life transformation, because it's:

Relational
Learner-to-learner interaction enhances learning and builds Christian friendships.

Experiential
What learners experience through discussion and action sticks with them up to 9 times longer than what they simply hear or read.

Applicable
The aim of Christian education is to equip learners to be both hearers and doers of God's Word.

Learner-based
Learners understand and retain more when the learning process takes into consideration how they learn best.

Group

Group's Dinner and a Movie: Chick Flicks

Visit our Web site: **www.group.com**

Credits

Contributing Authors: Cristine E. Arnold, Linda Crawford, Kate S. Holburn, and Louise A. Hughes

Editor: Amber Van Schooneveld

Creative Development Editor: Amy Nappa

Chief Creative Officer: Joani Schultz

Copy Editor: Kate Nickel

Art Director/Cover Art Director/Designer: Joey Rusk

Print Production Artist: Joyce Douglas

Cover Photographer: Rodney Stewart

Illustrator: Alan Flinn

Production Manager: DeAnne Lear

Library of Congress Cataloging-in-Publication Data
Group's dinner and a movie : chick flicks : friendship, faith, and fun for women's groups.
    p. cm.
ISBN 978-0-7644-3114-2 (pbk. : alk. paper)
0-7644-3114-5
1. Female friendship--Religious aspects--Christianity. 2. Small groups. 3. Motion pictures--Religious aspects--Christianity. 4. Film criticism.
    BV4647.F7G76 2006
    253'.7--dc22
                                                            2006000721

10 9 8 7 6 5 4 3   15 14 13 12 11 10 09 08 07
Printed in the United States of America.

Table of Contents

Introduction

Sometimes there's just nothing better than a good meal shared with good friends followed by a great movie. That's what *Group's Dinner and a Movie: Chick Flicks* is all about. You'll invite girlfriends over, prepare and enjoy a meal, and then watch and discuss a "chick flick" together. What could be more fun?

Chatting with girlfriends while chopping, stirring, and eating together can encourage some of the most enriching discussions you'll ever have. We've included Mealtime TalkStarters to get you all talking about the themes in the movies you'll be watching.

Before each event, read through the ingredients list and recipes. Serving sizes vary from recipe to recipe, so make sure to plan accordingly, and ask women to volunteer to bring different ingredients. If a recipe has a "make ahead" icon beside it, it either takes a little longer to make or is a good recipe for someone to bring already prepared.

All the movies we've selected contain deep spiritual themes that are applicable to any woman's daily life. We'll see betrayal, regret, love, and redemption. These themes can powerfully teach us about the God we serve and how to follow him better. There are discussion questions for you to use after each movie to get your group really thinking about the themes and ways to apply the lessons to everyday life. We've also included Bible verses that will get you started in the right direction.

We want this to be a complete experience women won't forget, so we've included decoration ideas for turning your cozy little dining and living rooms into a tropical beach, a fine Southern sitting room, and even a soccer field! There are also ideas in the Decorations section for fun items or clothing for women to bring with them, so let women know ahead of time what crazy hats or jewelry they'll be needing *this* time!

These events are great anytime. You can have a Dinner and a Movie once a quarter, once a month, or any time your group would enjoy something a little different.

We hope you enjoy these Dinner and a Movie events! Start the show!

Is It Legal to Show These Movies to My Small Group?

In general, federal copyright laws do allow you to use videos or DVDs for the purpose of home viewing as long as you aren't charging admission. However, you may feel more comfortable if you purchase a license. Your church can obtain a license from Christian Video Licensing International for a small fee. Just visit www.cvli.org or call 1-888-302-6020 for more information. When using a movie that is not covered by the license, we recommend directly contacting the movie studio to seek permission to use it.

Come join us for

Chick **Flicks**

We'll Watch

Fried Green Tomatoes

WHEN: _____
TIME: _____
WHERE: _____
_____
_____
RSVP: _____

Come join us for

Chick **Flicks**

We'll Watch

While You Were Sleeping

WHEN: _____
TIME: _____
WHERE: _____
_____
_____
RSVP: _____

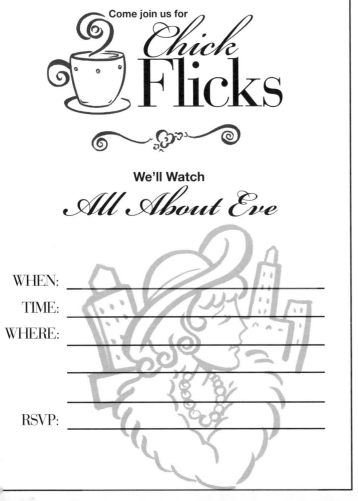

Come join us for

Chick **Flicks**

We'll Watch

All About Eve

WHEN: _____
TIME: _____
WHERE: _____
_____
_____
RSVP: _____

Come join us for

Chick **Flicks**

We'll Watch

Steel Magnolias

WHEN: _____
TIME: _____
WHERE: _____
_____
_____
RSVP: _____

Come join us for

Chick Flicks

We'll Watch
Sense and Sensibility

WHEN: _____

TIME: _____

WHERE: _____

_____

RSVP: _____

Come join us for

Chick Flicks

We'll Watch
13 Going On 30

WHEN: _____

TIME: _____

WHERE: _____

_____

RSVP: _____

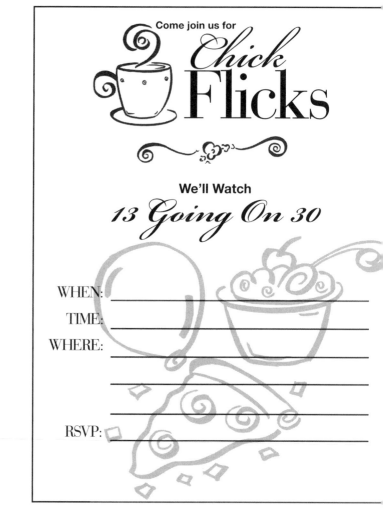

Come join us for

Chick Flicks

We'll Watch
Little Women

WHEN: _____

TIME: _____

WHERE: _____

_____

RSVP: _____

Come join us for

Chick Flicks

We'll Watch
Casablanca

WHEN: _____

TIME: _____

WHERE: _____

_____

RSVP: _____

Come join us for

Chick
Flicks

We'll Watch
The Princess Bride

WHEN: _____

TIME: _____

WHERE: _____

_____

_____

RSVP: _____

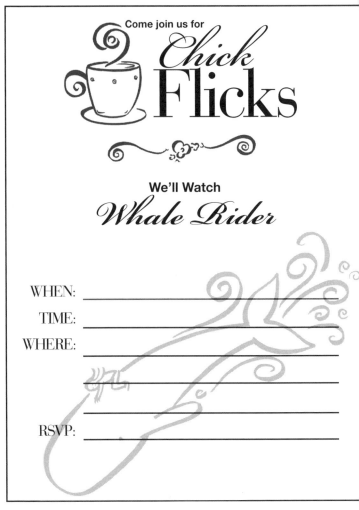

Come join us for

Chick
Flicks

We'll Watch
Whale Rider

WHEN: _____

TIME: _____

WHERE: _____

_____

_____

RSVP: _____

Come join us for

Chick
Flicks

We'll Watch
Enchanted April

WHEN: _____

TIME: _____

WHERE: _____

_____

_____

RSVP: _____

Come join us for

Chick
Flicks

We'll Watch
Bend It Like Beckham

WHEN: _____

TIME: _____

WHERE: _____

_____

_____

RSVP: _____

Fried Green Tomatoes

Genre: Drama   **Length:** 130 minutes   **Rating:** PG-13

QUICK PLOT: *An unhappy housewife becomes friends with an elderly lady who regales her with the remarkable tale of a special friendship.*

DINNER
"Secret's in the Sauce" Sandwiches
Fried Green Tomatoes
Deviled Eggs
Beverages (iced tea, lemonade, water)

MOVIE SNACKS

Whistle Stop Old-Fashioned Peach Cobbler
Vanilla Ice Cream

❧ SUPPLIES ❧

Before your Dinner and a Movie event, you may want to talk to everyone in the group and divide the ingredients list. Keep in mind that some items, such as the pork roast for the sandwiches, cost a lot more than others. Perhaps two people would like to share the cost of the roast, while others can each bring a couple of items.

What you'll need: *Names:*

Make Ahead of Time

"Secret's in the Sauce" Sandwiches (recipe on page 11)

Fried Green Tomatoes

4 medium, firm green tomatoes

1/4 cup milk

2 eggs, beaten

1/4 cup flour

1 cup cornmeal or fine dry bread crumbs

1/2 cup bacon grease or vegetable oil

salt and pepper

Deviled Eggs

6 hard-boiled eggs

1/4 cup mayonnaise

2 teaspoons spicy brown mustard

1 teaspoon horseradish sauce

salt and pepper

paprika

Whistle Stop Old-Fashioned Peach Cobbler

two 15-ounce cans sliced peaches

1/2 teaspoon cinnamon

6 tablespoons butter

1/2 cup sugar

1/4 cup packed brown sugar

1 cup flour

2 teaspoons baking powder

1/4 teaspoon salt

1 cup milk

Extras

vanilla ice cream

beverages

Easy Option Meal

OK, so the idea of a being a pampered Southern belle appeals more to you than sweating in a Southern kitchen. We can accommodate. It's hard to get more Southern than barbecue, so go to the supermarket and pick up some kaiser rolls and a tub of shredded barbecue beef. Combine it with side dishes from the deli, such as potato salad, corn on the cob, or green beans. Some fast-food restaurants and delis offer more Southern fare, such as sweet potato dishes, fried okra, and corn bread. Mix and match for something simple, easy, and kitchen-free.

RECIPES

 Make Ahead of Time

"SECRET'S IN THE SAUCE" SANDWICHES

3- to 4-pound boneless pork shoulder roast

2 medium onions, sliced

1 1/2 to 2 cups bottled barbecue sauce

1/2 teaspoon hot pepper sauce

2 tablespoons orange marmalade (or 1 tablespoon packed brown sugar)

1 tablespoon cornstarch

1 tablespoon cold water

8 to 10 sandwich buns

Cut roast into large cubes, 2- to 3-inches square. Place in slow cooker with onions. In a bowl, mix barbecue sauce, marmalade, and hot pepper sauce. Pour over meat and onions. Cover and cook on low for 8 to 10 hours or until meat is cooked through and tender. Remove pork and onions from the slow cooker with a slotted spoon, and place on tray or plate. Shred the pork with a fork and set aside.

Combine cornstarch and cold water until completely blended. Turn slow cooker on high, and add cornstarch mixture to juices in slow cooker. Blend well. Cover and cook on high for 1 minute. Return pork and onions to slow cooker, stir to coat well, and then cook on high for 10 minutes. Add more barbecue sauce if desired. (If it will be a while before you eat, return the slow cooker to low to keep warm and tilt the lid to vent the steam.)

To serve, spoon a generous amount of pork and onions onto sandwich buns. Serve with extra barbecue sauce and horseradish sauce, if desired. Serves 8 to 10 people.

FRIED GREEN TOMATOES

4 medium, firm green tomatoes

1/4 cup milk

2 eggs, beaten

1/4 cup flour

1 cup cornmeal or fine dry bread crumbs

salt and pepper

1/2 cup bacon grease or vegetable oil

Cut unpeeled tomatoes into thin slices, no more than 1/2-inch thick. Mix milk and eggs in a bowl. Mix flour and cornmeal or bread crumbs in another bowl. Pat tomato slices dry with a paper towel, sprinkle with salt and pepper, and then dip into egg mixture. Let excess egg mixture drip off, and then coat well with cornmeal or crumb mixture. Heat the grease or oil thoroughly over medium-high heat before placing tomatoes in pan. Fry tomatoes in the skillet with hot grease or oil until browned, turning gently after 3 to 5 minutes. Serves 6 to 8.

 Helpful Hint

Place cooked tomatoes on a stack of 2 or 3 paper towels for 1 to 2 minutes before placing them on your serving plate. This will allow some of the grease to be absorbed and keep them crispy longer. If fried tomatoes sounds a bit too heavy, cook tomatoes using a low-fat cooking spray instead.

Decorations

Put a little of the South into your living room and a little Whistle Stop into your kitchen to give your guests a warm, Southern welcome. Gather country-style items, such as stitched quilts, throws, lace doilies, a nice tea set on a platter, or even that old rocking chair in the back room. Arrange the items around the room in which you'll watch the movie to transform it into a genteel Southern sitting room.

Turn your kitchen into a cafe by hanging some old-style restaurant signs with phrases like "Fried Green Tomatoes… Served Hot," "Fresh Cobbler," and "Ice Cold Lemonade." You can find signs made out of tin or wood at craft stores. Or make the signs yourself using your computer or by drawing them by hand. Don't forget to put down a checkered tablecloth or place mats to finish the look.

Then ask your friends to dress up in their best Southern style. They can come as grand as a Southern belle or wear rolled up jeans like Idgie, but impress upon them the dire need for a hat…the bigger and more ostentatious the better.

RECIPES

DEVILED EGGS

6 hard-boiled eggs

1/4 cup mayonnaise

2 teaspoons spicy brown mustard

1 teaspoon horseradish sauce

salt and pepper

paprika

Peel, rinse, and pat dry hard-boiled eggs. Cut each egg in half lengthwise and remove yolks. Place yolks in a bowl and mash with a fork or pastry cutter. Add mayonnaise, brown mustard, and horseradish sauce and mix well. Season with salt and pepper if desired. Place approximately 1 rounded teaspoon of yolk mixture into each half egg white. Sprinkle with paprika for garnish. Serves 6.

WHISTLE STOP OLD-FASHIONED PEACH COBBLER

two 15-ounce cans sliced peaches, drained well

1/2 teaspoon cinnamon

6 tablespoons butter

1/2 cup sugar

1/4 cup packed brown sugar

1 cup flour

2 teaspoons baking powder

1/4 teaspoon salt

1 cup milk

This rich, easy-to-make, old-fashioned-style cobbler is fantastic over vanilla ice cream.

Preheat oven to 350 degrees. Drain the peaches and sprinkle them with cinnamon. Stir until peaches are coated; then set aside. In a 2-quart baking dish, melt butter. In a separate bowl, combine sugar, brown sugar, flour, baking powder, and salt. Add milk and stir until mixed. Pour batter over butter in baking dish. Do *not* stir. Spoon peaches evenly over the batter. Again, do *not* stir. Bake for 1 hour. Let cool for 10 to 15 minutes before serving. Serves 6 to 8.

Helpful Hint

For a stronger peach flavor, use 3 cups fresh peaches peeled and sliced, mixed with 1/2 cup sugar, instead of canned peaches. Or for an easy, healthy alternative, simply serve fresh peach slices over light vanilla ice cream.

COOKING TOGETHER

1. There will be plenty to do when everyone arrives, so have the ladies set their hats aside and roll up their sleeves. Have one volunteer put together the peach cobbler according to the instructions, and place it in the oven to bake.

2. Have one or two volunteers prepare the deviled eggs according to the recipe on page 12.

3. Slice the green tomatoes, and start cooking them according to the recipe on page 11.

4. When the deviled eggs and tomatoes are nearly ready, have another person prepare a sandwich for each woman. Have her place the finished sandwiches on a plate or platter. Cover the sandwiches with aluminum foil to keep them warm.

5. Have those who are not busy cooking set the table. Be sure to set out the extra barbecue sauce, horseradish sauce, and extra napkins. They can also prepare drinks for everyone.

6. When everything is finished, place the food on the table and have everyone gather around. Ask someone to pray, and then enjoy your home-cooked Southern meal! (And don't worry about the cobbler. The oven timer will let you know when it is finished. Just pull it out of the oven and let it cool while you finish dinner and clean up.)

7. You could play the martyred Southern hostess and have your guests leave the dishes for you to clean up later, but what are friends for if not to help you with life's little messes? Ask two people to clear the table, one or two people to be in charge of putting away the leftovers, and two people to rinse off the dishes and put them in the dishwasher (or set them aside to wash later). You will find that cleanup is done in much less than a Southern minute, without a perfectly coiffed hair out of place!

Mealtime TalkStarters

- The South loves its fried foods. What is the strangest thing you have ever eaten fried?

- As women, we truly relish attention lavished on us by the one we love the most. What is the most outrageous thing you've ever done to attract the attention of the opposite sex?

- Why do you think so many women struggle with issues of self-esteem?

- How important or unimportant is it for us to conform to the lifestyle society expects of us?

LET'S WATCH A MOVIE!

Fried Green Tomatoes

THE PRE-SHOW

Have everyone gather in your new Southern sitting room where you will show the movie. When everyone is gathered, serve up the warm cobbler and ice cream to anyone who wants dessert. (If the cobbler isn't finished cooking or cooling, simply save dessert for the Post-Show!) Don't forget to allow a quick restroom break.

Pass out pens and sheets of paper to your guests to write down their answers to the quiz. We all know that food is a big part of Southern culture. Take this Comfort Food Trivia Quiz to see who is the true Southern belle.

COMFORT FOOD TRIVIA QUIZ

1. How many pigs does a typical American eat in a lifetime?
   a. 8   b. 28   c. 48

2. What fine, Southern lady brought us the first ready-mix food to ever be sold commercially?

3. What is the most popular meal ordered in sit-down restaurants in the United States?

4. What woods should you never use to barbecue as they can add harmful tar and resins to food?

5. What are grits?

6. What popular packaged treat was invented in 1931 as a way to use the thousands of shortcake pans that sat empty all year except for strawberry season?

7. Why is pound cake called pound cake?

Answers

1. b. 28

2. Aunt Jemima brought us pancake flour in 1889.

3. Fried chicken

4. Pine, spruce, or other evergreen wood should never be used to barbeque. Only hardwoods, such as hickory or mesquite, should be used.

5. Coarsely ground corn or hominy boiled in water and eaten for breakfast.

6. Hostess Twinkies

7. Traditional pound cake contained a pound of butter, a pound of sugar, a pound of eggs, and a pound of flour. This made it easy for illiterate cooks to remember the recipe!

THE SHOW
Fried Green Tomatoes

Genre: Drama

Length: 130 minutes

Rating: PG-13 for language and mature themes

Plot: Evelyn Couch (Kathy Bates) is a discouraged and unhappy housewife seeking some kind of meaning in her life when she happens upon Ninny Threadgoode (Jessica Tandy), an elderly but spry woman living at a nursing home. Evelyn and Ninny's relationship blossoms into deep friendship as Ninny tells Evelyn the monumental story of the friendship between Idgie Threadgoode and Ruth Jamison.

Evelyn is enraptured as Idgie and Ruth's story, set in 1920s Alabama, unfolds. It is full of passion, laughter, tragedy, courage, and determination (and a little murder mystery thrown in for good measure). Evelyn's self-confidence grows along with her friendship to Ninny. As she learns more about herself and the life she wants to lead, she realizes how incredible true friendships are.

THE POST-SHOW

After the movie, use some or all of these questions to discuss the spiritual themes in *Fried Green Tomatoes*.

What was Evelyn searching for beyond a more satisfying relationship with her husband?

Should we gain all our fulfillment through our significant relationships? If not, what else is there? Have you felt that you're "missing something" even when you have loving relationships?

Why do you think Buddy's death took such a toll on Idgie Threadgoode? How do you suppose her life would have been different if Buddy were still alive?

There are two key friendships in this movie. What do you think drew these women together? What made their friendships so special?

What do you think of Evelyn's response to having her parking space taken? Why do you think we let things build up so much that little things like this set us off? How can we prevent this?

Share your opinion of Frank Bennett. How do you think Christians should respond to people like Frank?

What lessons about friendship can we learn from this movie and apply to our own lives?

Bible Passages
You may want to use these Bible passages during your movie discussion:

- John 15:12-13—The greatest love is sacrificial.

- 1 Corinthians 4:6-7—One man is not greater than another.

- Romans 12:2—Do not conform to the ways of this world.

- James 1:12—Blessed are those who persevere.

PRAYER

End the evening with prayers for strength, courage, and perseverance. Ask for prayer requests from individuals about situations or daily struggles where strength, courage, and perseverance are needed in their lives. Ask God to help your group practice true friendship and help all to put into practice the lessons learned from *Fried Green Tomatoes*.

While You Were Sleeping

Genre: Romantic Comedy   **Length:** 103 minutes   **Rating:** PG

QUICK PLOT: *Lucy, a lonely subway employee, saves the life of a handsome stranger who now lies in a coma. Mistaken for his fiancée, she gains a family and much more.*

DINNER
Pot Roast
Mary's Creamy Mashed Potatoes
Dinner Rolls
Green Bean Casserole
Beverages (hot tea, coffee, or ice water)

MOVIE SNACKS
Ice Cream Kitties
"We Promise It's Not Elsie's" Eggnog

 SUPPLIES

Before your Dinner and a Movie event, you may want to talk to everyone in the group and divide the ingredients list. In honor of Lucy's holiday meal with the Callaghans, we suggest pot roast and mashed potatoes. Keep in mind that some items, such as the pot roast, cost more than others. Perhaps two people would like to share the cost of the roast, while others can bring a couple of items.

What you'll need: *Names:*

Make Ahead of Time **Pot Roast** (recipe on page 19)

Mary's Creamy Mashed Potatoes

6 medium all-purpose potatoes   _____

3/4 cup milk   _____

1/2 stick butter or margarine   _____

Green Bean Casserole

1 can cream of mushroom soup   _____

three 14-ounce cans cooked green beans   _____

1/2 cup milk   _____

1 1/3 cups french fried onions   _____

Make Ahead of Time **"We Promise It's Not Elsie's" Eggnog** (recipe on page 20)

Ice Cream Kitties

2 or 3 half-gallon containers
of ice cream in a variety of flavors   _____

1 package chocolate sandwich cookies   _____

one 8-ounce package M&M's candies   _____

whipped topping   _____

1 package black licorice laces   _____

Extras

1 package brown 'n' serve rolls   _____

1 stick butter   _____

beverages   _____

Easy Option Meal

If the thought of cooking a big holiday meal makes you want to hop the next flight out of town, you're in luck. The deli section of most supermarkets carries almost anything you would want to make a holiday dinner on the sly. Pick up a roasted chicken, sides of mashed potatoes and gravy, and a vegetable or salad dish. You may even find they have green bean casserole. Slide over to the bread aisle and pick up a bag of ready-made dinner rolls, and you are set.

RECIPES

Make Ahead of Time
POT ROAST

With this simple recipe, the roast cooks all day and makes its own gravy.

- one 3- to 4-pound chuck roast
- 1 small onion chopped
- one 16-ounce package baby carrots
- 1 cup water
- 1 can cream of mushroom soup
- 1 package dry onion soup mix
- 1 tablespoon Worcestershire sauce

Mix cream of mushroom soup, onion soup mix, water, and Worcestershire sauce in a bowl and set aside. Place baby carrots and onion in the bottom of a slow cooker. (If you are using a heavy pot, such as a Dutch oven, place the vegetables around the sides of roast.) Place roast on top of vegetables, and pour sauce mixture over the meat. Following the slow cooker manufacturer's instructions, cook on low approximately 8 to 10 hours. (For a Dutch oven, cook approximately 3 to 4 hours.) Meat should easily shred or fall apart with a fork when done. Serves 6 to 8.

MARY'S CREAMY MASHED POTATOES

Mary is Jack's little sister who mashed the potatoes for Lucy's dinner with the Callaghans.

- 6 medium all-purpose potatoes
- 1/2 to 3/4 cup hot milk
- 1/2 stick butter or margarine
- salt

Peel potatoes and dice into 1-inch cubes. (For variety, you can leave half of the skins on the potatoes.) Place diced potatoes in a large saucepan, and cover with cold water. Bring to a boil, and boil gently for about 20 minutes or until you can mash a cube easily with a fork. Drain well. Add hot milk and butter, and mash with potato masher or fork until lumps are smoothed out. Transfer to a serving bowl, add salt to taste, and whip with a whisk or fork until fluffy. Add additional hot milk if necessary. (For a change of pace and richer flavor you can substitute 6 to 8 ounces of cream cheese in place of the butter. Cut up the softened cream cheese before adding it to the potatoes.) Makes approximately 6 servings.

GREEN BEAN CASSEROLE

- 1 can cream of mushroom soup
- three 14-ounce cans cooked green beans, drained
- 1/2 cup milk
- pepper
- 1 1/3 cups french fried onions

Preheat oven to 350 degrees. Mix the soup, milk, and pepper to taste in a 1 1/2-quart baking or casserole dish. Add the green beans and 2/3 cup of the fried onions, and stir until just coated. Bake for 25 minutes. Top with remaining 2/3 cup fried onions, and bake for an additional 5 minutes or until onions are lightly browned. Makes approximately 6 servings.

Decorations

Since this movie takes place during the Christmas season, this may be the perfect opportunity for you to indulge in that childhood fantasy of "Christmas in July." Dust off those Christmas decorations, reindeer mugs, and star-shaped plates and go to town! You can even put up an artificial tree if you're *really* feeling the holiday spirit.

To keep the decorating simple, put up a few strings of Christmas lights around a window or an archway. Drape red and green cloth or paper napkins over end tables and flat surfaces. Place holiday-scented votive candles around the room to light just before your guests arrive. Play your favorite Christmas music in the background.

As a fun twist to tie in the movie, encourage your guests to dress as doctors, nurses, or even patients (although you may want to discourage hospital gowns!). Purchase some inexpensive surgical or allergy masks at your local pharmacy to give to your guests. Create hospital badges with your guests' names, their pictures, and an "official" title, such as Registered Nurse, Doctor of Oncology, or, for that friend with the great sense of humor, Head of Psychiatric Ward.

RECIPES

Make Ahead of Time

"WE PROMISE IT'S NOT ELSIE'S" EGGNOG

Elsie's eggnog proved more alcohol than eggnog. This creamy recipe uses rum extract instead of rum.

6 beaten egg yolks	1 1/2 teaspoons rum extract
1/4 teaspoon salt	1 tablespoon vanilla
1 cup sugar	2 cups heavy whipping cream
3 cups milk	nutmeg

In a large, heavy saucepan, mix egg yolks, salt, milk, and 5 tablespoons of sugar. Cook and stir continuously over medium heat until mixture just coats a metal spoon with a thin whitish or beige film. Do not boil. Remove from heat. Place the pan in a bowl of ice water, and stir for 2 or 3 minutes to cool. Stir in rum extract, vanilla, and 3 tablespoons sugar until sugar is completely dissolved and incorporated. Cover and chill for 4 to 24 hours.

Just before guests arrive, beat whipping cream and remaining 1/2 cup sugar in a mixing bowl until soft peaks form. Transfer the chilled egg mixture into a serving or punch bowl. Fold in whipped cream. Cover and chill. Stir lightly before serving. Sprinkle each serving with nutmeg. Makes about ten 4-ounce servings.

ICE CREAM KITTIES

This fun dessert was created from a variety of things that appear in the movie. While watching the movie, see how many references you can find to ice cream, cats, and Oreo cookies.

2 or 3 half-gallon containers of ice cream in a variety of flavors	1 container spray whipped topping or whipped cream
1 package chocolate sandwich cookies	1 package black licorice laces cut in 4- or 5-inch strips
one 8-ounce package M&M's candies	

To create your cat, place a baseball-sized ball of ice cream in a bowl. (Tip: Let the ice cream sit out for a bit to soften; then use an extra large ice cream scoop.) Take 2 cookies and push them halfway into the ice cream about an inch apart at the top of the ice cream ball. These are the cat's ears. Shake the whipped cream container well and place two silver-dollar dollops of whipped cream next to each other halfway down the "face" of your cat. These are the cheeks. Take 2 M&M's for eyes and 1 for the nose, and place them accordingly. Take 2 to 3 black licorice laces per side for the cat's whiskers, and poke them into the whipped cream cheeks, making sure you push them into the ice cream also so they will stand out.

Feel free to get creative. You can add stripes with chocolate sauce or "fur" with different colored sprinkles, but most of all, have fun! Serves approximately 8, depending on how much ice cream you eat!

Helpful Hint

If a guest is preparing the eggnog in advance, you may want to advise her to make the whipped cream when she arrives so it will stay fresh.

COOKING TOGETHER

1. Before everyone arrives, make the whipped cream and complete the eggnog according to the recipe instructions.

2. When everyone arrives, have someone chop and peel the potatoes and begin to boil them.

3. While the potatoes are being peeled, have someone else prepare the green bean casserole according to the recipe and place it in the oven.

4. Ask someone to set the dinner rolls on a baking sheet and cover them with foil or plastic wrap until the casserole is finished cooking.

5. Invite the remaining guests to set the table using your fun holiday dishes and prepare drinks for everyone.

6. When the casserole is finished and cooling, remove the foil or plastic wrap from the rolls, and bake them according to the package instructions.

7. While the rolls are cooking, have someone dish up the pot roast, vegetables, and gravy into a serving dish and place it on the table.

8. Place the remaining food on the table, and have your guests gather around. Ask someone to pray over the meal. Then enjoy your holiday feast!

9. Cleanup after a holiday meal is much simpler with some good-humored help. Ask two women to clear the table, one or two others to be in charge of putting away the leftovers, and two to rinse the dishes and put them in the dishwasher. (Or one to wash and one to dry if you don't have a dishwasher.) You can even all croon your favorite holiday tunes together, and cleanup will be done in a snap!

10. Before you start the movie, set out the eggnog and the ingredients for the Ice Cream Kitties for guests to assemble their treats.

Mealtime TalkStarters

- Share your favorite holiday memory or tradition.

- Have you ever had a crush on someone you've never met? If so, tell everyone about it.

- Why do you think we develop attractions to people we don't know?

- What are good ways to respond to loneliness?

LET'S WATCH A MOVIE!

While You Were Sleeping

THE PRE-SHOW

After the meal and cleanup, gather the ingredients for the Ice Cream Kitties on the table. Hand out a festive Christmas bowl to each guest who wants to make a kitty. Enjoy yourselves while making your own creative desserts.

When everyone has her dessert, gather in the room where you'll be showing the movie. Pass out pens and paper for your guests to write down their answers to the trivia questions. Read the questions aloud. When everyone has finished writing, read the correct answers and vote on who has the best "wrong" answer. Then serve eggnog to those who want some, and enjoy the movie!

SANDRA BULLOCK TRIVIA QUIZ

1. For whom was the role of Lucy in *While You Were Sleeping* originally written?
  - a.   Demi Moore
  - b.   Meg Ryan
  - c.   Julia Roberts

2. In what action movie did Bullock make her on-screen debut?
  - a.   *Speed*
  - b.   *Hangmen*
  - c.   *Demolition Man*

3. What writer is one of Sandra Bullock's favorites?
  - a.   Ernest Hemingway
  - b.   Tom Clancy
  - c.   Dr. Seuss

4. Sandra and her father work together on a passion of Sandra's. What is it?
  - a.   Real estate
  - b.   Deep-sea fishing
  - c.   Jujitsu

5. What is the most outrageous thing Bullock has done for a role to date?
  - a.   Bungee jumped
  - b.   Duct-taped her breasts
  - c.   Shaved her head

 Answers

1. a. Demi Moore

2. b. *Hangmen* in 1987

3. c. Dr. Seuss—She has his entire collection.

4. a. Real estate—They buy and renovate old homes.

5. b. She taped her chest with duct tape (ouch!) for a love scene to make sure nothing showed.

THE SHOW
While You Were Sleeping

Genre: Romantic Comedy

Length: 103 minutes

Rating: PG for some language

Plot: Sandra Bullock plays Lucy Moderatz, a lonely subway attendant who has fallen in love with Peter Callaghan (Peter Gallagher), a man she has never met but sees often through her tollbooth. When Peter is mugged, Lucy saves his life, but he sustains injuries that put him in a coma.

Suddenly, Lucy's solitary life is filled to the brim when Peter's family mistakes her for Peter's fiancée and embraces her as one of their own. Lucy finds herself falling in love not only with the Callaghan family but with Jack, Peter's brother, as well.

When Peter finally regains consciousness, Lucy knows that the moment of truth is close at hand. She must decide between the man she's always thought she could love, the man she's beginning to love, and the truth.

THE POST-SHOW

At the conclusion of the movie, use some or all of these questions to discuss the spiritual themes in *While You Were Sleeping*.

❓ What struck you about Lucy's reaction as she watched the Callaghan family open gifts and celebrate Christmas?

❓ How important is it to feel like you belong to something bigger than yourself?

❓ Discuss Lucy's decision to go along with the assumption that she was Peter's fiancée. Was it justifiable? Why or why not?

❓ What do you admire about the way Lucy handled her loneliness? How do you deal with everyday life when you've had a loss?

❓ As Christians, what can we learn from *While You Were Sleeping* about how God takes care of our needs and desires?

❓ Why do you think Peter pushed himself so far away from his family? Why do we sometimes push ourselves away from those closest to us?

❓ In what small ways does this movie show us how we should be conscious of what makes us happy and fulfilled?

❓ How do you imagine the events in this movie would have changed the characters over time? How has an unusual occurrence in your life shaped who you are?

Bible Passages
You may want to use these Bible passages during your movie discussion:

- 2 Corinthians 4:2-3—Tell the truth.

- Galatians 5:7-10—Do not be deceived; obey the truth.

- Matthew 6:25-34—God will take care of us.

- 1 John 3:1-2—We are children of God.

Prayer

End the evening with a prayer of thanksgiving. Ask the members of your group to write down the names of people who are special and close to them. Gather and ask each woman to picture special people in her mind. Say a prayer thanking the Lord for the lovely people he places in our lives, and ask him to bless them as he has blessed us.

All About Eve

Genre: Drama   **Length:** 138 minutes   **Rating:** Unrated

QUICK PLOT: *An aging actress faces betrayal, love, career uncertainty, and the challenge of growing old gracefully.*

DINNER
New York Strip Steak
Salad
Baked Potatoes
Beverages (sparkling cider, ice tea, or ice water)

MOVIE SNACKS
New York Cheesecake
Italian Sodas

 SUPPLIES

Before your Dinner and a Movie event, you may want to talk to everyone in the small group and divide the ingredients list. Keep in mind that some items, such as steak, cost a lot more than others. Perhaps several people would like to share the cost of the steak, while others each bring a couple of items.

What you'll need: *Names:*

New York Strip Steak
   one 4- to 6-ounce New York strip steak,
     1 inch thick per person   _____

1 tablespoon extra virgin olive oil per person   _____

1 clove garlic, minced per person   _____

1/2 teaspoon ground cinnamon per person   _____

1/2 teaspoon white sugar per person   _____

2 tablespoons apricot preserves per person   _____

salt   _____

pepper   _____

Baked Potatoes
   1 potato per person   _____

sour cream   _____

butter   _____

Extras
   one 6-ounce bag of lettuce for every 4 to 6 people   _____

salad fixings, such as croutons,
   chopped vegetables, and dressings   _____

beverages   _____

inexpensive faux-pearl and
   faux-diamond necklaces (optional)   _____

 Make Ahead of Time

New York Cheesecake (recipe on page 27)

Italian Sodas (recipe on page 28)

Easy Option Meal

You can have an easy meal in honor of the setting of this movie, the Big Apple, in a New York minute. Pick up a meal of hot dogs and french fries at a local fast-food restaurant. Make them "Coney Island" dogs by topping them with chili, mustard, and chopped onions. Or pick up deli sandwiches, such as Reubens, and potato chips at a grocery store. Buy a pre-made frozen cheesecake for dessert.

 # RECIPES

NEW YORK STRIP STEAK

one 4- to 6-ounce New York strip steak, 1 inch thick per person

1 tablespoon extra virgin olive oil per person

1 clove garlic, minced per person

1/2 teaspoon ground cinnamon per person

1/2 teaspoon white sugar per person

2 tablespoons apricot preserves per person

salt

pepper

Combine olive oil, garlic, cinnamon, sugar, and apricot preserves in a small bowl and mix well. Make several shallow cuts in both sides of each steak; then lightly sprinkle steaks with salt and pepper. Put steaks and sauce together in a dish. Coat the steaks with the sauce; then refrigerate for at least 60 minutes.

Turn grill on high. Grill steaks until done (about 10 minutes), flipping occasionally.

BAKED POTATOES

1 potato per person

sour cream

butter

Preheat oven to 450 degrees. Scrub potatoes with a brush and water to remove all dirt, and then pierce each potato with a fork. Place directly on the oven rack and bake 1 hour for large potatoes, 50 minutes for medium potatoes, and 40 to 45 minutes for small potatoes. To check if the potatoes are done, squeeze to see if they feel soft. You may also test with the sharp point of a knife. Break apart with a fork and garnish with butter, sour cream, or whatever else you choose.

 ## NEW YORK CHEESECAKE

Make Ahead of Time

15 graham crackers, crushed

2 tablespoons butter

four 8-ounce packages cream cheese

1 1/2 cups white sugar

3/4 cup milk

4 eggs

1 cup sour cream

1 tablespoon vanilla extract

1/4 cup all-purpose flour

Preheat oven to 350 degrees. Melt butter and mix with graham cracker crumbs in a medium-sized bowl. Place mixture in 9-inch greased pan, pressing into bottom of pan. In another bowl, mix together cream cheese and sugar until smooth. Blend in milk. Mix in the eggs one at a time; then mix in sour cream, vanilla, and flour. Mix until smooth. Pour filling into pan on top of the crust. Bake for 1 hour. If possible, let cake cool in oven (turned off) for a few hours. Chill in refrigerator before serving. Makes 12 servings.

Decorations

To achieve a sophisticated New York atmosphere, decorate for this event with a black-and-white theme. Drape black and white curtains, drapes, and other lengths of cloth around the dining room. You can hang the material from the light fixtures, from chairs, or arrange in an artistic way on other surfaces. Add white Christmas lights around the room for a festive touch.

Cover half the dining table with a black tablecloth and the other half with a white tablecloth. Use black and white stir straws to embellish everyone's drink glasses, and look for black and white paper plates, cups, and napkins.

Scatter black vases filled with real or fake white flowers around the room. Black and white candles and candleholders will also add a great touch to the dining room. Make a sign that says "Now Showing: *All About Eve*," and hang it on the wall. You can make this sign very simple or give it Broadway flair by outlining the sign with a string of white twinkle lights. Also, cut out black and white cardboard stars and place them around the room or hang them on the walls.

Ask women to come wearing any (real or fake) fur coats or wraps they might have.

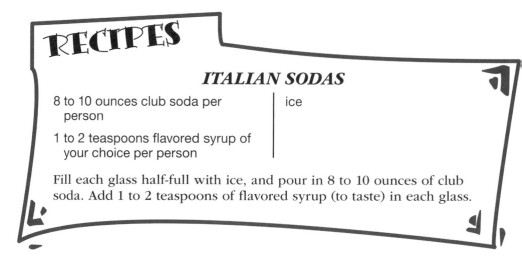

RECIPES

ITALIAN SODAS

8 to 10 ounces club soda per person

1 to 2 teaspoons flavored syrup of your choice per person

ice

Fill each glass half-full with ice, and pour in 8 to 10 ounces of club soda. Add 1 to 2 teaspoons of flavored syrup (to taste) in each glass.

Mealtime TalkStarters

- If you could spend two days in New York, what would you do? Or tell about a time you visited New York.

- Tell about a theater experience you've had (your favorite show, the most boring, the most outrageous). What do you think is so appealing about make-believe?

- What's an award you've received or have always wanted to receive? What does it take to get that award? Is it worth it?

- Whom do you admire most in the world, and why? Tell about a time you started a friendship with someone you admired or who admired you.

COOKING TOGETHER

1. Before the group arrives, marinate the steaks in the refrigerator for at least 1 hour. Put the scrubbed potatoes in the oven at least 30 minutes before everyone arrives.

2. As each woman arrives, give her an inexpensive faux-pearl or faux-diamond necklace to don. You can pick these up at a costume shop or dollar store. Women can take them home to serve as a reminder of their true worth and beauty in God's eyes.

3. When everyone has arrived, invite volunteers to prepare the Italian sodas according to the recipe above. Put the sodas in the refrigerator to keep cold for later.

4. Ask a volunteer to put the steaks on the grill and flip them occasionally, cooking each for about 10 minutes or until they've reached desired doneness. Have another volunteer prepare the salad by mixing together lettuce and salad fixings, such as carrots, cucumbers, tomatoes, cheese, and croutons in a large bowl. Put in the refrigerator.

5. Have those who aren't busy cooking set the table. They can also set out salad dressing, salt, pepper, butter, and sour cream. Then they can prepare drinks for everyone.

6. Have someone monitor the baked potatoes and take them out when they're done (1 hour for large potatoes, 50 minutes for medium potatoes, and 40 to 45 minutes for small potatoes). See recipe on page 27 for how to test whether or not the potatoes are done.

7. When all is ready, set the potatoes, steak, and salad on the table. Have everyone gather at the table. Ask someone to pray over the food. Then enjoy the meal!

8. Work together to clear the table and clean the dishes you used (or you may set the dishes aside and wash them later). Put any leftovers in the refrigerator.

9. Serve the Italian sodas with cheesecake during the movie. See recipes above and on page 27.

LET'S WATCH A MOVIE!

All About Eve

THE PRE-SHOW

Have everyone gather in the area where you'll show the movie. If you have just finished eating dinner together, you may want to provide a quick restroom break.

When everyone has gathered, serve cheesecake and Italian sodas to anyone who wants dessert. Be sure to provide napkins (black and white napkins would be very appropriate).

Hand out paper and pens, and have everyone answer these fun trivia questions about classic black-and-white movies. Then see how everyone did! Invite women to discuss their favorite classic films—black-and-white or color.

CLASSIC MOVIE TRIVIA QUIZ

1. What movie, often considered one of the best movies in cinematic history, did Orson Welles star in, co-write, and direct?

2. *Grapes of Wrath* is based on a novel by what author?

3. What's the name of George Bailey's visiting angel in *It's a Wonderful Life*?

4. What famous line ends *Casablanca*?

5. What actor starred in the 1936 movie *Modern Times*?

6. What movie starred Katharine Hepburn as a socialite divorced from Cary Grant's character and pursued by Jimmy Stewart's character?

 Answers

1. *Citizen Kane*
2. John Steinbeck
3. Clarence
4. "Louis, I think this is the beginning of a beautiful friendship."
5. Charlie Chaplin
6. *The Philadelphia Story*

THE SHOW
All About Eve

Genre: Drama

Length: 138 minutes

Rating: Unrated. However characters drink, smoke, and there are minor sexual themes (subtle innuendos, and a hint at adultery).

Plot: Bette Davis is Margo Channing, a successful Broadway actress. Margo has great friends who care about her but are often hurt by her cynicism, bitter insecurities, and avoidance of true intimacy. Margo struggles with growing older—not believing anyone could love her unconditionally.

After one night's performance, an adoring fan, Eve Harrington (Anne Baxter) is introduced to Margo. Margo is flattered by the admiration, and Eve slowly works her way into Margo's life.

But Margo's fragile ego can't handle the strain of the constant presence of one so lovely and young—Eve is the epitome of what she used to be.

The actions of the women in the film offer both surprising and sobering insight into ambition, betrayal, and power—as well as revealing the power of true friendship, unconditional love, personal identity, and self-worth.

THE POST-SHOW

After the movie, use some or all of these questions to discuss the spiritual themes in *All About Eve*.

What does this movie reveal about how insecurities affect us and those we love? Can you give an example of this from your own life?

Often our outward identities don't reflect our true selves. What outward trappings do you rely on for your identity? How does this differ from the real you?

How can we really know who we are? From what should we derive our identities? How can we be content with who we are?

How easy or difficult is it for you to believe in your own worth? to accept God's unconditional love?

How would you describe the way Margo and her relationships were transformed at the end of the movie? Tell about a time God used pain or hurt to transform you for the better.

What qualities do you look for in a friend? How do you decide to trust a friend, despite the risk of being hurt?

When have you been lied to, hurt, or betrayed by someone? How did you react? What happened? Explain.

What do you imagine happened to Eve, Margo, and her friends next? How can we apply the insights we've gained from the movie to our lives?

Bible Passages
You may want to use these Bible passages during your movie discussion:

• Proverbs 31:30—Beauty is fleeting.

• 1 Peter 3:3-4—Beauty comes from what's inside.

• John 15:9-17—Jesus is an unfailing friend.

• Psalm 139:14—We are wonderfully made.

Prayer

End the evening by praying together. Ask for prayer requests. Encourage each person to share one specific way to put into practice the lessons learned from *All About Eve*. Have each person pray for the woman sitting to her right. Tell women to take home their necklaces as a reminder of their true worth and beauty in God's eyes.

Steel Magnolias

Genre: Drama   **Length:** 117 Minutes   **Rating:** PG

QUICK PLOT: *In a small Louisiana town, a close-knit group of friends gathers at Truvy's Beauty Parlor to share gossip and to support each other through life's triumphs and tragedies.*

DINNER
Easy Option Meal
Beverages (soda, ice tea, or ice water)

SUPPLIES

This Dinner and a Movie event will be a little out of the ordinary. Every woman needs time out of the kitchen and deserves some pampering! So instead of cooking together, you'll treat yourselves to a night at the beauty salon! Use the Easy Option Meal, and assign volunteers to pick up your dinner items. Everyone can split the cost of the meal. Have your group divide the supply list for putting together your beauty stations. Women can bring items from home to reduce the expense. If you have women in your group who are in the beauty business, ask if they would volunteer to help organize and run the stations. Use the included fun beauty "recipes" or come up with your own!

Easy Option Meal

Keep it simple so you have more time for pampering! Pick up a Southern meal of fried chicken from your favorite fast-food restaurant or grocery-store deli. Order a complete meal with mashed potatoes, rolls, and salad, or buy them separately. Serve with ice tea or water. You can use plastic plates, cups, and utensils for quick cleanup. For dessert, buy a ready-made pecan pie.

What you'll need:

Names:

Truvy's Hair Spot
set(s) of hot rollers _____

curling iron(s) _____

hairbrushes and combs (new or have them bring their own) _____

bobby pins _____

decorative hair accessories _____

hairspray _____

Truvy's Nail Spot
assorted nail polish _____

nail polish remover _____

nail files (1 per person) _____

cotton balls or pads _____

Truvy's Makeup Spot
hand mirrors _____

assorted colors of eye shadow _____

assorted blushes _____

assorted lipstick shades _____

cotton swabs _____

makeup removal cloths _____

Truvy's Sugar Scrub (instructions on page 35) _____

Truvy's Lip Gloss (instructions on page 35) _____

Truvy's Bath Salts (instructions on page 35) _____

Make Ahead of Time

RECIPES

TRUVY'S SUGAR SCRUB

1/4 cup sugar

2 tablespoons oil (canola or olive)

1 drop scented oil (optional)

In a small bowl, mix the sugar and oil. Add one drop of scented oil, such as a lemon or floral oil, if desired. To use, put 1 to 2 teaspoons on hands and rub all over backs of hands, palms, and fingers. Rinse with warm water, and pat hands dry on a towel. Leaves hands silky smooth!

TRUVY'S LIP GLOSS

1 tablespoon petroleum jelly

1/2 to 1 teaspoon crushed powder eye shadow

cosmetic glitter (optional)

Combine the petroleum jelly, eye shadow, and glitter. Use a cotton swab to dab on lips. Try different shades of eye shadows for fun!

TRUVY'S BATH SALTS

2 cups Epsom salts

scented oils

food coloring (optional)

Mix Epsom salts with a drop or two of scented oil and food coloring. Make ahead or have each woman make her own with 1/4 to 1/3 cup of salts. Place finished bath salts in small jars or bags to take home.

Decorations

Take a trip to Truvy's Beauty Parlor! Decorate your space like a beauty salon complete with stations set up for hair, nails, and makeup. Arrange chairs near tables or dressers set up with beauty supplies. Have women bring their favorite nail polish, makeup, and hair supplies. (See supplies list.)

Try an "everything pink" theme for your salon. Use pink plastic tablecloths to cover your station tables, pink towels, and pink flowers and accessories. You can ask women to come dressed in shades of pink, and gather some fun pink accessories for dress up, such as hats, boas, gloves, jewelry, and hair accessories.

Place copies of the beauty "recipes" at each station for the women to follow. Encourage them to also have fun experimenting and helping each other with hairstyles, nail polish, and makeup! You might want to find inspirational photos of hair and makeup and set them at the stations to get the creative juices flowing. Cut pictures out of magazines or print them off of the Internet. Think Dolly Parton, Delta Burke—even Scarlett O'Hara!

Be sure to have plenty of mirrors available and a camera for makeover photos. If you have a digital camera, you can even print out a group photo for each woman to take home! Send women home with a package of Truvy's Bath Salts to remind them to take time for pampering in the upcoming week (instructions above).

Mealtime TalkStarters

- Tell a story of a beauty or hair disaster you've experienced.

- Talk about some of the different hairstyles you have tried, and how the culture, celebrities, or styles of the time influenced you.

- Share about how difficult or easy it is for you to take time to pamper yourself.

- Reveal your favorite beauty tip!

SALON TIME TOGETHER

1. Before your group arrives, arrange tables and chairs to make three beauty stations: Truvy's Hair Spot, Nail Spot, and Makeup Spot. Have some paper and cloth towels available at each station.

2. As they arrive, invite the women to place their beauty supplies at the appropriate stations. It might be helpful to assign a helper for each station to organize and set up the supplies and plug in the appliances.

3. Have other volunteers set up the dinner items. Use paper or plastic plates and cups and plastic silverware to make cleanup quick and easy.

4. Gather your group for dinner, and have someone pray over the meal and your time together. The meal time will be casual and unstructured—the women may sit in a few different areas to eat, or they can stand and move around talking with one another. Give them a few Mealtime TalkStarters to help generate conversation.

5. After everyone is done eating, clean up, and then take "before" pictures of each woman if you have a camera.

6. If your group is large enough, separate into three groups, and have each group spend about 10 minutes at each station. If you have a smaller group, you can do all of the stations together. Give a brief explanation of each station. At the hair station, women will be competing in a "Truvy Jones Hair Contest"—the bigger the better! Tell them to tease, curl, pin, and accessorize to their Southern hearts' content. Remind them, the higher the hair, the closer to God!

7. At the nail station, women can try Truvy's Sugar Scrub to soften their hardworking hands and then decorate their nails with fun new polish colors.

8. At the makeup station, have each woman mix up some of Truvy's Lip Gloss to match her eye shadow.

9. When you've gone through each station, make yourselves true divas with the fun boas, jewelry, and hats you've set out. End your salon time by showing off your new looks and sharing with each other how it felt to have some fun, pampered "girl" time. Vote for the winner of the "Truvy Jones Hair Contest," and be sure to get some pictures!

LET'S WATCH A MOVIE!

Steel Magnolias

THE PRE-SHOW

Gather in the area where you'll show the movie. Allow time for a quick restroom break.

After everyone has gathered, refill drinks and put out the pecan pie for those who would like dessert. Hand out pens and paper to each person, and have them answer these trivia questions about Julia Roberts, one of the stars in *Steel Magnolias*. Then see how everyone did!

JULIA ROBERTS TRIVIA QUIZ

1. What was Julia Roberts' first name before she changed it to Julia?

2. What movie launched her career success and earned her an Academy Award nomination?

3. Julia Roberts was the first actress to earn what salary for her role in *Erin Brockovich*?

4. What is Julia's true hair color?

5. What special event did Julia celebrate in 2004?

6. Why was a 9,000-year-old skeleton excavated in Bulgaria given the name "Julia Roberts" by archaeologists?

 Answers

1. Julia Roberts was born Julie Fiona Roberts.
2. *Pretty Woman*
3. $20 million
4. Dark blonde
5. The birth of her twins
6. The skeleton reportedly had perfect teeth and would have had Julia's perfect smile.

THE SHOW
Steel Magnolias

Genre: Drama

Length: 117 minutes

Rating: PG for language and brief nudity (locker room scene).

Plot: Truvy's Beauty Parlor is the gathering place for a close-knit group of women living in a small town. They share gossip and friendship as they support each other through life's joyful and tragic events.

Julia Roberts plays Shelby, the independent-minded daughter of M'Lynn (Sally Field). M'Lynn struggles to find a balance between being overprotective and supportive of her daughter when Shelby makes a choice that jeopardizes her health.

Shelby and M'Lynn's quirky and funny friends are there through the joy and sorrow of their lives. Together they explore and expound on the topics of love, death, aging, friendships, and hope.

THE POST-SHOW

After the movie use some or all of these questions to discuss the spiritual themes in *Steel Magnolias*.

- Which character from the movie do you most identify with, and why?

- What are some of the relationship challenges Shelby and her mother faced in the movie?

- What are some of the relationship challenges the women faced as friends? How are these similar to challenges you've faced with your friends?

- How do you feel Christianity was portrayed by the characters in this movie?

- Shelby said, "I'd rather have 30 minutes of wonderful than a lifetime of nothing special." How do you feel about her statement? Do you agree or disagree with her reasoning?

- Why do you think Shelby made the choice she did, even though she knew the dangerous consequences?

- How do you feel M'Lynn handled Shelby's death?

- Talk about your close friends and the ways they have supported you in difficult times.

Bible Passages
You may want to use these Bible passages during your movie discussion:

- Romans 12:15—Rejoice and mourn with friends.

- Proverbs 17:17—Love friends in adversity.

- Galatians 5:13-15—Love others as yourself.

PRAYER

End your night by joining in prayer. Have women pair up to pray for each other's prayer requests, and then get back together for a group prayer. Pray for friendships that will support and encourage the women in your group through shared laughter and shared tears. Make sure each woman takes home a bag of Truvy's Bath Salts to remind her to be thankful for her friends and to pamper herself!

Sense and Sensibility

Genre: Drama/Comedy/Romance   **Length:** 136 Minutes   **Rating:** PG

QUICK PLOT: *Mrs. Dashwood and her three daughters, Elinor, Marianne, and Margaret, experience poverty, heartbreak, and love after the death of their husband and father.*

DINNER
Roast Beef With Yorkshire Pudding
Sugar Snap Peas
Vanilla Pudding Trifle
Beverages (soda, milk, ice tea, or ice water)

MOVIE SNACKS
Currant-Cream Scones
Honey-Mint Coolers

 SUPPLIES

Before your Dinner and a Movie event, you may want to talk to everyone in the small group and divide the ingredients list. Keep in mind that some items, such as roast beef, cost a lot more than others. Perhaps two people would like to share the cost of the roast beef, while others each bring a couple of items.

What you'll need: *Names:*

Roast Beef With Yorkshire Pudding
one 2 1/2- to 3-pound rump roast

2 eggs

1 cup milk

1 cup all-purpose flour

3/4 teaspoon salt

3/4 teaspoon pepper

Sugar Snap Peas
1 cup fresh sugar snap peas per person

Vanilla Pudding Trifle
1 pre-made shortcake cup per person

1/2 of a 14-ounce can mixed fruit cocktail per person

pre-made vanilla pudding
    (4 ounces per person or 1 snack cup per person)

whipped topping (optional)

colored sprinkles (optional)

Extras
instant beef gravy

beverages

canned whipped cream

strawberry jam

 Make Ahead of Time
Currant-Cream Scones (recipe on page 42)

Honey-Mint Coolers (recipe on page 42)

Easy Option Meal

If your group isn't inclined to cook, pick up a quick and easy meal of roast beef sandwiches from a local fast-food restaurant or deli. You may also buy frozen peas and packaged shortbread cookies or scones and canned whipped cream from the grocery store.

RECIPES

ROAST BEEF WITH YORKSHIRE PUDDING

one 2 1/2- to 3-pound rump roast	1 cup all-purpose flour
2 eggs	3/4 teaspoon salt
1 cup milk	3/4 teaspoon pepper

Heat oven to 450 degrees. Wipe rump roast with a damp paper towel; then rub with salt and pepper. Place on rack in roasting pan; then roast in oven for 25 minutes. Reduce heat to 300 degrees, and cook until internal temperature reaches 150 degrees (rare), 160 degrees (medium), or 170 degrees (well-done). Cooking time can vary from 1 to 2 hours, depending on desired doneness. Remove from oven and tent with foil to keep warm.

Turn the oven up to 450 degrees and pour the pan drippings from the rump roast into an 11x7 or 9x9-inch pan. *Do not use a glass pan.* Place the pan in the oven to keep sizzling while you prepare the batter. Combine the eggs, milk, flour, pepper, and salt and beat until blended. Pour batter into the prepared pan and bake for 25 to 30 minutes. Serve a square of Yorkshire pudding with each helping of roast beef. Prepare instant gravy per package directions and serve with roast beef and Yorkshire pudding. Serves approximately 8 to 10 people.

SUGAR SNAP PEAS

Put sugar snap peas in a pot about two-thirds full of water. Bring water to a boil; then lower heat and let simmer for about 5 minutes (or until desired tenderness is reached). Drain peas and serve.

VANILLA PUDDING TRIFLE

1 pre-made shortcake cup per person	vanilla pudding (instant or pre-packaged)
1/2 of a 14-ounce can mixed fruit cocktail per person	whipped topping (optional)
	colored sprinkles (optional)

For each person, place 1 pre-made shortcake cup in the bottom of a bowl. Cover with 1/2 can of mixed fruit cocktail, including some juice. Top this with 1 serving of vanilla pudding (about 4 ounces or 1 pre-packaged cup). You may garnish with whipped topping and colored sprinkles.

Decorations

Decorate for this event with an English countryside theme. Purchase or gather colorful yet inexpensive flowers and put them around the dining room in vases or decorative teapots. You can also set out beautiful silk flowers and plants.

Hang inexpensive paintings and other framed pieces around your dining-room table to achieve an artistic elegance. Place a white linen or lace tablecloth on the table. Scatter lit candles around the room. If you're able to find candelabras or nice candleholders, use them as well.

Purchase inexpensive hats or bonnets for everyone to wear, or encourage everyone to bring a beautiful hat. You can also drape a bonnet or sun hat on the back of each chair before the group arrives.

If possible, use dishes or paper plates with a flower pattern, and purchase inexpensive decorative napkins. Play piano or classical music in the background during the meal preparation and dinner.

RECIPES

Make Ahead of Time

CURRANT-CREAM SCONES

2 cups all-purpose flour	4 tablespoons butter
2 teaspoons baking powder	2 eggs, well beaten
1 tablespoon sugar	1/2 cup half-and-half
1/2 teaspoon salt	1/2 cup currants

For 5 minutes, soak currants in enough hot water to barely cover. Drain well. Preheat oven to 425 degrees. Grease a cookie sheet. Mix flour, baking powder, sugar, and salt in a large bowl. Use a pastry blender or your hands to work the butter into the mixture until it resembles a coarse meal. Stir in the eggs and half-and-half until blended. Stir in the currants.

Turn out onto a floured board and knead for about one minute. Form dough into a 7-inch circle. Cut into 12 wedges. Place on cookie sheet and bake for 15 minutes. Serve with whipped cream and strawberry jam. Makes 12 scones.

HONEY-MINT COOLERS

4 tablespoons clear honey	2 cups water
16 mint leaves	8 ice cubes
juice from 2 lemons	4 mint sprigs (for garnish)

Combine ingredients in blender and mix on maximum speed for about 40 seconds. Then pour into cups to serve. If you'd like, decorate cups with mint sprigs. Serves 4.

COOKING TOGETHER

1. Before the group arrives, begin cooking the roast beef in the oven.

2. Blend the ingredients for the Yorkshire pudding; then begin cooking the Yorkshire pudding (total cook time will be about 25 to 30 minutes).

3. When everyone arrives, invite volunteers to prepare the peas and the Vanilla Pudding Trifle according to the recipes on page 41. Also have a volunteer prepare Honey-Mint Coolers according to the recipe on page 42. Put the Honey-Mint Coolers in the refrigerator to keep cold for later.

4. Have those who aren't busy cooking set the table with plates, silverware, and napkins. Set out gravy, salt, and pepper. Have someone prepare drinks for everyone. Begin a pot of hot English Breakfast tea so it's ready to drink during the movie.

5. When the roast beef and Yorkshire pudding are done, dinner is ready and everyone can prepare a plate of food.

6. Invite everyone to gather at the table. Ask someone to pray over the meal; then enjoy!

7. When finished, work together to clear the table and clean the dishes you used (or you may set the dishes aside for now and wash them later). Put any leftovers in the refrigerator.

8. Serve the Honey-Mint Coolers with Currant-Cream Scones during the movie. See recipes on page 42.

Mealtime TalkStarters

- Would you have liked living in early 19th-century England? Why or why not?

- If others were to describe you in one word, what would it be?

- If you could describe yourself in one word, what would it be?

- How can we be hurt by other people's expectations of us? by the standards we set for ourselves?

- How would you describe the balance between being wise and practical and being spontaneous and taking chances? When have you had to learn this balance in your life?

LET'S WATCH A MOVIE!

Sense and Sensibility

THE PRE-SHOW

Have everyone gather in the area where you'll show the movie. If you have just finished eating dinner together, you may want to provide a quick break for people to use the restroom.

When everyone has gathered, serve the Currant-Cream Scones, English Breakfast tea, and Honey-Mint Coolers to anyone who wants dessert. Be sure to provide napkins (decorative would add the perfect touch). Hand out paper and pens, and have everyone answer these fun trivia questions about actors who appear in *Sense and Sensibility*—Emma Thompson, Hugh Grant, Kate Winslet, and Alan Rickman.

Then read the answers aloud and see how everyone did! Invite everyone to discuss their favorite movies in which any of these actors starred.

Sense and Sensibility
ACTORS TRIVIA QUIZ

1. Which *Sense and Sensibility* actor played a villain opposite Bruce Willis in his or her first major film?

2. Emma Thompson won a Best Adapted Screenplay Oscar for *Sense and Sensibility* in 1995. For what movie did she win an Oscar for Best Actress?

3. What was the name of the young aristocrat Kate Winslet played in the 1997 blockbuster *Titanic*?

4. What *Sense and Sensibility* actor fought with Colin Firth, kissed Julia Roberts, and was prime minister?

5. Which three actors starred together in both *Sense and Sensibility* and the 2003 comedy *Love Actually*?

6. In *About a Boy*, what song does Hugh Grant's character Will sing onstage during a school talent show?

Answers

1. Alan Rickman

2. *Howard's End* in 1992

3. Rose DeWitt Bukater

4. Hugh Grant. He had a fight scene with Colin Firth in *Bridget Jones' Diary*, kissed Julia Roberts in *Notting Hill*, and played the prime minister in *Love Actually*.

5. Emma Thompson, Hugh Grant, and Alan Rickman

6. "Killing Me Softly"

The Show
Sense and Sensibility

Genre: Drama/Comedy/Romance

Length: 136 minutes

Rating: PG for mild thematic elements

Plot: When Mr. Dashwood dies, law dictates he can leave only a small portion of his estate to his second wife (Gemma Jones) and three daughters—sensible Elinor (Emma Thompson), passionate Marianne (Kate Winslet), and imaginative Margaret (Emilie Francois). In 19th-century England, the family's lack of money diminishes any hope of the Dashwood daughters marrying well.

Two sisters, Marianne and Elinor, both find love, but each takes a very different approach to it. Marianne is rescued by the dashing John Willoughby (Greg Wise) and passionately gives her heart to him, while the wealthy but mysterious Colonel Brandon (Alan Rickman) loves her from afar. And Elinor struggles with being the practical member of the family while developing strong feelings for rich Edward Ferrars (Hugh Grant), whose family forbids him to pursue Elinor.

The Dashwood women journey through it all—hardship, romance, sickness, and love—with an abundance of grace and humor, and learn the balance that must exist between sense and sensibility.

The Post-Show

After the movie, use some or all of these questions to discuss the spiritual themes in *Sense and Sensibility*.

 Tell about a time you observed someone handle hardship or loss with humor—or a time you did.

How is prejudice against the poor obvious in our society today? As Christians, how should we treat the poor? What actions can you take?

To which character in this movie do you relate the most? Why?

At the end of the movie, Marianne talks about the choice of marrying for love or money. Do you agree or disagree with her? Explain.

Tell about a time you had a moment like Elinor's outpouring of emotion when she finds out Edward is not married after all.

When should we be open with others about our feelings? When should we hide our true emotions?

Marianne gave her heart to Willoughby and was devastated when he abandoned her. But she found a true and selfless love in Colonel Brandon. When have you not gotten what you wanted only to be grateful later?

As Christians, how can we discern between what seems exciting and what God gives that is truly best for us?

What examples of grace did you see in this movie? How would you describe grace? How is grace reflected in a person's life?

Bible Passages
You may want to use these Bible passages during your movie discussion:

- Proverbs 14:20-21—Be kind to the needy.

- Romans 12:11-13—Serve God with hope, patience, and faith.

- 1 Corinthians 13:1-13—True love is unconditional.

- James 1:12—Persevere through hardship.

PRAYER

End the evening by praying together. Ask for prayer requests. Encourage each person to share one specific way to put into practice the lessons learned from *Sense and Sensibility*. Have each person pray for someone else in the group. For example, everyone could pray for the person with the birthday that directly follows hers chronologically.

13 Going On 30

Genre: Romantic Comedy **Length:** 98 Minutes **Rating:** PG-13

QUICK PLOT: *A 13-year-old girl makes a wish on her birthday and wakes up as a 30-year-old woman who finds she has a lot of making up to do for the lost years!*

DINNER
Thriller Pizza
Thirty-Flirty Salad
Beverages (soda, lemonade, or ice water)

MOVIE SNACKS
Second-Chance Sundaes
Assorted Candy

SUPPLIES

Before your Dinner and a Movie event, you may want to talk to the women in your small group and divide the ingredients list. This meal is all about having fun making choices! You will need women to bring one or two ingredients that can be used both as a pizza topping and a salad mix-in. You will need others to bring toppings for the sundaes. In addition to assigning the ingredients, have women bring some of their favorite candy to share for movie-time snacks.

What you'll need: Names:

Thriller Pizza
1 large prepared pizza crust per 4 people   _____

one 16-ounce jar of pizza sauce per pizza   _____

one 12-ounce bag of shredded pizza cheese per pizza   _____

Thirty-Flirty Salad
one 6-ounce bag of salad lettuce per 4 to 6 people   _____

salad dressings (at least 3 choices)   _____

Toppings for Thriller Pizza and Thirty-Flirty Salad
meats, such as pepperoni, ham, bacon   _____

fruits and veggies, such as pineapples, black olives,
fresh spinach, green peppers, onions, fresh mushrooms   _____

Second-Chance Sundaes
vanilla ice cream (1 quart per 6 people)   _____

chocolate syrup   _____

whipped cream (pre-made frozen or canned)   _____

nuts   _____

colored sprinkles   _____

maraschino cherries (1 bottle)   _____

birthday candles (1 per person)   _____

Extras
party-favor bags (1 per person)   _____

beverages   _____

assorted candy   _____

Easy Option Meal
For a fun and easy alternative to cooking, order delivery or take-out pizza with a variety of toppings and pick up assorted salads at your local grocery store's deli. Buy a few flavors of individual ice cream cups and chocolate sauce for the dessert sundaes.

Easy Tip
For a lighter meal, purchase some low-fat or sugar-free toppings, salad dressings, and ice cream.

RECIPES

THRILLER PIZZA

1 large prepared pizza crust per 4 people

one 16-ounce jar of pizza sauce per pizza

one 12-ounce bag of shredded pizza cheese per pizza

assorted toppings

Preheat oven to baking temperature recommended on pizza crust package. Place pizza crust on large pizza pan. Spread pizza sauce evenly over crust. Prepare toppings by shredding or chopping into chunky pieces, and place each choice in a small bowl. Assign four people per pizza, and have each woman choose and add toppings for her portion of the pizza. Top with cheese and bake according to pizza crust directions. Use pizza cutter to cut into individual slices, and serve with Thirty-Flirty Salad.

THIRTY-FLIRTY SALAD

one 6-ounce bag of salad lettuce per 4 to 6 people

assorted toppings

assorted salad dressings

Empty bags of lettuce into a large salad bowl. Arrange small bowls of toppings (left over from pizza preparation) and salad dressings buffet-style next to lettuce. Allow each person to create her own salad with the toppings and dressing of her choice.

SECOND-CHANCE SUNDAES

vanilla ice cream (1 quart per 6 people)

chocolate syrup

whipped cream (pre-made frozen or canned)

nuts

colored sprinkles

maraschino cherries (1 bottle)

birthday candles (1 per person)

After the movie, set out ice-cream topping choices with serving spoons. Scoop ice cream into individual dishes, and allow each person to build her own sundae. Place a birthday candle on top of each sundae, and have each woman pray a quick silent prayer and blow out the candle before eating!

Decorations

Decorate for this event to create the atmosphere of a teenage birthday slumber party. Hang colored streamers and balloons, and use birthday-themed paper plates, cups, and napkins. Decorate your table with colorful paper or a plastic tablecloth, or use a Twister mat instead for fun. (Don't forget to wipe it clean first!) For added sparkle, sprinkle the table with glitter or confetti.

Use traditional games such as Life and Battleship as added decorative pieces and conversation starters. Ask each woman to bring her favorite fluffy pillow or stuffed animal. Arrange these in groups throughout the room.

Ask people to bring copies of their high school or middle school yearbooks or photos if they have them. Set up a table to display the yearbooks and photos, and spend time laughing and sharing memories while the pizza is cooking!

Encourage everyone to dress like they did at 13. For added fun, take "updated teen" photos to distribute at a later date. (If you use a digital camera, you can print them out after the movie or e-mail them later.)

Play some fun, upbeat music in the background from the '50s, '60s, '70s or '80s, depending on the average age of your group. Or turn on a radio station that plays them all!

COOKING TOGETHER

Mealtime TalkStarters

- Tell about yourself and your interests when you were 13 years old.

- Describe how when you were 13 you pictured your life would be now.

- Tonight's meal was all about making choices! Discuss what factors influenced your decisions to choose your pizza and salad toppings, and how this is like or unlike the process of making choices in life.

- Share how the Christian influences you had—or did not have—when you were younger affected your choices at the time. How about now?

1. Before your group arrives, set out cutting boards, knives, a large salad bowl, a large bowl for candy, pizza pans, and multiple small serving bowls.

2. As people arrive, have them place their candy in the large bowl and their yearbooks, stuffed animals, and other items in designated areas.

3. Preheat the oven according to the pizza crust directions, and begin preparing the pizza and salad toppings. Designate a few people to prepare the pizza crusts with sauce, and have others chop and place the toppings in individual serving bowls.

4. Have another person place the lettuce in a bowl and set out salad dressings.

5. To assemble the pizzas, gather your group and assign four women to a pizza. Have each person choose and place her desired toppings on her portion of the pizza. Encourage each group to share with each other why they like or dislike certain toppings and how their tastes have changed (or not changed) since they were younger.

6. Arrange the leftover toppings buffet-style next to the bowl of lettuce and salad dressings.

7. Place the pizzas in the preheated oven and set a timer for the recommended time on the crust package. If cooking multiple pizzas at one time, it is a good idea to rotate the pizzas on the oven racks (top to bottom, bottom to top) halfway through the cooking time.

8. While the pizzas are cooking, have everyone gather around the memorabilia table and giggle over high school or middle school pictures and memories.

9. When the pizzas are done, use a pizza cutter to cut individual slices and serve. Have each person prepare her salad, pick up a drink, and gather at the table. Ask someone to pray over the meal, and enjoy!

10. Cleanup is a breeze! Toss paper plates, napkins, and cups in the trash, and place leftovers in the refrigerator.

11. Save the Second-Chance Sundaes for dessert and discussion time *after* the movie. (See the Post-Show instructions.)

LET'S WATCH A MOVIE!

13 Going On 30

THE PRE-SHOW

Have each woman fill a party-favor bag with candy from the candy bowl, gather up her pillow or stuffed animal, and meet in the area where you'll watch the movie together. Be sure to allow time for a restroom break!

Designate one person to lead the trivia quiz and keep score, and have the group form two teams. Make sure participants know that they are free to be a little wild and silly. (It wouldn't be a slumber party otherwise!) Tell them to shout out the answers as fast as they can. The team that gets the most correct answers gets to "toss" their pillows and stuffed animals at the other team! Beware: This may start an all-out pillow fight!

TRIVIA QUIZ

1. What was the original title of *13 Going On 30*?
   a. *Sparkle*
   b. *Sugar and Spice*
   c. *Turn Back Time*

2. What was the most popular girl's name of the '70s and '80s?

3. In what country was the title changed to *Suddenly 30* because the distributors thought audiences would misunderstand the original title?

4. In what year did Cosmopolitan magazine get its start?
   a. 1886
   b. 1946
   c. 1966

5. What was Jennifer Garner's first major in college before switching to drama?

6. In what decade did Mattel introduce the first Barbie Dream House?

Answers

1. b. *Sugar and Spice*
2. Jennifer
3. Australia
4. a. 1886. It began as a magazine "for the whole family."
5. Chemistry
6. The 1960s. 1962 to be exact. It sold for $5.79 in the 1962 Montgomery Ward catalog.

THE SHOW
13 Going On 30

Genre: Romantic Comedy

Length: 98 minutes

Rating: PG-13 for some sexual content and brief drug references.

Plot: Jennifer Garner stars as Jenna Rink, a 13-year-old girl with a wish to be "30, flirty, and thriving"—just like the women in the hip fashion magazines she reads. Striving to fit in with the popular crowd, she invites the cool "six chicks" from school to her 13th birthday party.

But the party is a disaster. A humiliated Jenna locks herself in the closet and makes a fateful wish—to be grown up with the life she's always wanted! She emerges from the closet to find herself a beautiful and successful 30-year-old. Her life is everything she thought she wanted.

Jenna embarks on a journey of self-discovery that requires her to experience the consequences of her past choices. Through love, laughter, and tears, she comes to realize what it is she *really* wants in life.

THE POST-SHOW

After the movie, set out the ice cream and sundae toppings buffet-style, and let everyone build her own sundae. Top each sundae with a birthday candle, and have each person say a silent "birthday" prayer before blowing out the candle and enjoying. During dessert, use some of these questions to discuss the spiritual themes in *13 Going On 30*.

What do you think is the main message of this movie?

How does this movie cause you to reflect on your own life?

How do you relate to Jenna's struggles at 13? as an adult?

Which peer pressures did Jenna face that were the same at age 13 as at 30? Which were different?

Jenna's mother felt her mistakes in life were what taught her how to correct them. Do you feel the same way about mistakes in your own life? Why or why not?

Jenna got a second chance to change her life. Do you think God gives us second chances? Why or why not?

As Christians, what lessons can we learn about what to value in life and how to make the best choices every day?

Bible Passages
You may want to use these Bible passages during your movie discussion:

- Proverbs 8:10-11—God's instructions are more valuable than gold.

- Jeremiah 29:11—God has good plans.

- Proverbs 22:1—Good character is worth more than riches.

PRAYER

After dessert and discussion, end the evening with prayer. Have the women form a circle and place their right hands in the center (as in a team cheer). Have each woman say a one-sentence prayer for a lesson she can apply to her life from *13 Going On 30*. At the end, raise your hands up in the center together in a group cheer. Try something fun, such as "Go girls! Go God!"

Little Women

Genre: Drama **Length:** 115 minutes **Rating:** PG

QUICK PLOT: *This story chronicles the lives of a mother, her four daughters, and their daily toils in the absence of their father during the Civil War.*

DINNER
Brunswick Stew
Orchard House Cornbread
Beverages (soda, ice tea, or ice water)

MOVIE SNACKS
Sister's Spice Cake
Hot Tea

SUPPLIES

Before your Dinner and a Movie event, you may want to talk to everyone in your group and divide the ingredients list. Have others make the cornbread and spice cake in advance. This meal is simple, delicious, and the stew is an authentic recipe from the Civil War era!

What you'll need: Names:

Easy Option Meal

Soups and stews were a mainstay of Early American cuisine, so if you don't have time to cook, simply pick up a beef and vegetable stew from the deli of a grocery store, or even buy a gourmet canned stew. Serve with your choice of bread—biscuits, cornbread, or rolls—and twice-baked potatoes that can be purchased at the deli and reheated at home. Buy a spice cake or loaf of banana bread for dessert and the meal is complete.

Brunswick Stew

1 tablespoon cooking oil _____

2 large onions, chopped _____

one 16-ounce can of lima beans _____

one 16-ounce can of corn _____

one 16-ounce can of chicken broth _____

1 pound of cooked chicken meat (or equivalent amount canned) _____

two 16-ounce cans of chopped tomatoes _____

3 cooked, peeled, and chopped potatoes _____

dash of pepper, garlic, brown sugar, and salt _____

hot sauce to taste _____

Extras

butter _____

honey _____

tea bags _____

sugar _____

cream _____

beverages _____

Make Ahead of Time **Orchard House Cornbread** (recipe on page 55) _____

Sister's Spice Cake (recipe on page 55) _____

RECIPES

BRUNSWICK STEW

Two or three communities in the Northeast with the name "Brunswick" like to claim this stew as their own creation, but generally Brunswick County, Virginia, is given the credit. Many believe this recipe was created in the early 1800s.

1 tablespoon cooking oil	two 16-ounce cans of chopped tomatoes
2 large onions, chopped	3 cooked, peeled, and chopped potatoes
one 16-ounce can of lima beans	
one 16-ounce can of corn	dash of pepper, garlic, brown sugar, and salt
one 16-ounce can of chicken broth	
1 pound of cooked chicken meat (or equivalent amount canned)	hot sauce to taste

Place the onions and a tablespoon of oil in a stockpot. Cook on low heat until the onions turn clear; then add the rest of the ingredients to the pot. Cover and increase heat until the stew is bubbling. Cook for 20 minutes, stirring often. Serves 4 to 6.

ORCHARD HOUSE CORNBREAD

1 cup flour	1/2 teaspoon salt
1 cup cornmeal	1/4 cup oil
1/4 cup sugar	1/2 cup milk
4 teaspoons baking powder	

Preheat oven to 425 degrees. In a medium bowl, use a mixer to blend all of the ingredients until smooth. Pour into a greased 9-inch round pan, and bake for approximately 20 minutes. Cool completely and cover with aluminum foil. Makes 6 to 8 servings.

SISTER'S SPICE CAKE

1 package spice cake mix	1/3 cup oil
3 eggs	1/2 cup powdered sugar
1 1/4 cup applesauce	

Preheat oven to 350 degrees. Grease and flour a 13x9-inch pan. Combine cake mix, eggs, applesauce, and oil in a bowl and beat at medium speed with an electric mixer for 2 minutes. Pour into pan and bake for 40 minutes or until a toothpick inserted in center comes out clean. Cool completely and cover with aluminum foil. If desired, sprinkle with powdered sugar before serving. Makes 12 servings.

Decorations

Have fun decorating for this event with an Early American theme: old photographs, flags, or Civil War memorabilia. Pull out those special items that your grandmother gave you from when she was young, and put them out as décor, such as quilts, gloves, brooches, and hats. Do you have some old dolls? Set them out on a bench or chair.

Use doilies as coasters around the dinner table. You can make pretty place card holders out of flowery paper and a calligraphy font on the computer. Fresh-cut flowers would make a beautiful centerpiece for the dinner table.

Have classical music or piano music playing softly in the background. To make it smell like a cozy Early American home on a chilly night, a spice-scented candle, such as cinnamon, would be perfect.

If you have an ornate tea set, plan on using it for dessert and teatime. Buy some pretty, flowery napkins to go with it.

COOKING TOGETHER

Mealtime TalkStarters

• Imagine what life was like in the 1800s. Discuss what it would have been like to be a woman during that time.

• What is one of your favorite old-fashioned family recipes that has been passed down to you? What does it remind you of?

• What was one of your favorite family dinners growing up?

• Is there a tradition you would like to see passed down through your children or other family members?

• Why is family special to you? How has God blessed you in your family?

1. Before guests arrive, chop the onions. They can be cooked earlier and refrigerated if convenient. Peel and cut the potatoes into small pieces, and soak them in water until you are ready to add them to the stew.

2. As guests arrive, add the ingredients for the stew to the pot, making sure that the heat isn't turned on until there is a liquid base in the pot. The potatoes need to go in right away so they are thoroughly cooked when it's time to eat.

3. Add the seasonings to the stew last. Have someone taste the stew and add more seasonings as needed.

4. Have someone cut the cornbread into wedges and put them on a serving tray. You may want to heat the bread just before the meal starts.

5. Ask another volunteer to set the table and place the butter and honey on the table for the cornbread.

6. Have someone else prepare drinks for everyone.

7. Invite everyone to gather at the table. Ask someone to pray over the meal, and enjoy!

8. When you're finished eating, put dishes away and refrigerate the leftovers.

9. Before watching the movie, boil a pot of water for tea. Dust the Sister's Spice Cake with powdered sugar, and then slice.

LET'S WATCH A MOVIE!

Little Women

THE PRE-SHOW

Have everyone gather in the area where you'll be showing the movie. If you have just finished eating, give time for a quick restroom break.

Once everyone has gathered, serve the Sister's Spice Cake and tea (use that fancy china) with fun Victorian floral napkins. Hand out paper and pens, and have everyone answer the trivia questions about the women involved in this film. Then see how everyone did! Invite women to discuss their favorite actresses from this film.

TRIVIA QUIZ

1. Susan Sarandon (Mrs. March) stars in what 1990 action/adventure movie with Geena Davis?

2. How old was Kirsten Dunst (younger Amy March) when *Little Women* hit theaters in 1994?

3. Winona Ryder (Jo March) was engaged in 2000 to what famous actor from Massachusetts?

4. What famous actress played the role of Jo in the original 1933 *Little Women*?

5. Who wrote the book this movie was based on?

6. True or false: The author wrote this story based on her own experiences growing up with three sisters.

Answers

1. *Thelma and Louise*
2. 12
3. Matt Damon
4. Katharine Hepburn
5. Louisa May Alcott
6. True

The Show
Little Women

Genre: Drama

Length: 115 minutes

Rating: PG, appropriate for families

Plot: With their father at the Civil War battlefront and their mother working hard to support the family, the four March sisters learn to rely on each other as they face life's challenges and learn to overcome their own personal weaknesses.

When their mother is called away to take care of their ailing father, they each find their roles within the family and society as they mature and learn to work together. Life isn't always easy, but these sisters make each day an adventure. They navigate their way through relationships—developing friendships and learning what it's like to fall in love—while realizing that the dynamics of their relationships with each other change along the way.

The Post-Show

After the movie, use some or all of these questions to discuss the spiritual themes in *Little Women*.

- Which character can you most identify with? Why?

- Which character would you most like to emulate? Why?

- Sometimes our families are a blessing, and sometimes they seem more like a curse, such as when Amy burned Jo's manuscript. How does God sharpen our characters when our families are not so easy to get along with? Give a specific example from your own life.

- Beth was known for her compassion for the poor. What are some practical ways can we reach out this week to those who are less fortunate than us?

- Mrs. March said, "I wish I could give my girls a more just world, but I know you'll make it a better place." How can we make the world a better place?

- Jo sold her hair so her mother could afford to go see her father. Think about a time you had to give up something dear to you for a loved one. What was it and how did it impact the other person?

- What is the one thing you can take from this movie and apply to your own life?

Bible Passages
You may want to use these Bible passages during your movie discussion:

- Colossians 3:12—Be patient, kind, and compassionate.

- Proverbs 22:6—Train children in the way they should go.

- Romans 12:18—Live at peace with others.

- Romans 12:10—Honor others before yourselves.

Prayer

End the evening by praying together. Ask for prayer requests. Encourage each person to share one specific way to put into practice the lessons learned from the movie *Little Women*. Have each person pray for someone else in the group.

Casablanca

Genre: Drama **Length:** 102 minutes **Rating:** PG

QUICK PLOT: *This classic World War II drama is a story of two men vying for the same woman's love against a backdrop of wartime conflicts.*

DINNER
Moroccan Chicken and Sweet Potato Stew
Casablanca Couscous
Melon Cubes
Beverages (soda, ice tea, or ice water)

MOVIE SNACKS
Coconut Almond Brittle
Cool Mint Tea

SUPPLIES

Before your Dinner and a Movie event, you may want to talk to the women in your small group and divide the ingredients list. Keep in mind that some items, such as the chicken and fruit, may cost more than others. Several women could share the cost of these ingredients, while others could bring one or two of the other items.

Easy Option Meal

If your group isn't inclined to cook, pick up lemon rotisserie chicken and some prepared couscous or tomato salads at your grocery store's deli. Accompany your meal with pita bread, pre-made hummus spreads, and pre-cut cantaloupe and watermelon cubes. Pick up some tasty baklava or coconut macaroons for dessert.

What you'll need: *Names:*

Moroccan Chicken and Sweet Potato Stew

6 boneless, skinless chicken thighs   _____

2 teaspoons extra virgin olive oil   _____

1 medium onion, thinly sliced   _____

1 tablespoon ground cumin   _____

1 teaspoon ground cinnamon   _____

one 14.5-ounce can of diced tomatoes with juice _____

one 15-ounce can of chickpeas (drained)   _____

one 14.5-ounce can of chicken broth   _____

1/2 cup orange juice   _____

1/4 teaspoon cayenne pepper (or to taste)   _____

one 29-ounce can cut sweet potatoes, drained and halved _____

3/4 cup pitted prunes (or 1 cup golden raisins)   _____

one 10-ounce package frozen chopped spinach (thawed) _____

2 tablespoons lemon juice   _____

Casablanca Couscous

1 box of couscous mix   _____

olive oil   _____

Extras

cantaloupe and watermelon (pre-cut cubes or whole) _____

beverages   _____

toothpicks   _____

 Make Ahead of Time

Coconut Almond Brittle (recipe on page 61)   _____

Cool Mint Tea (recipe on page 62)   _____

RECIPES

MOROCCAN CHICKEN AND SWEET POTATO STEW

6 boneless, skinless chicken thighs

2 teaspoons extra virgin olive oil

1 medium onion, thinly sliced

1 tablespoon ground cumin

1 teaspoon ground cinnamon

one 14.5-ounce can of diced tomatoes with juice

one 15-ounce can of chickpeas (drained)

one 14.5-ounce can of chicken broth

1/2 cup orange juice

1/4 teaspoon cayenne pepper (or to taste)

one 29-ounce can cut sweet potatoes, drained and halved

3/4 cup pitted prunes (or 1 cup golden raisins)

one 10-ounce package frozen chopped spinach (thawed)

2 tablespoons lemon juice

Over medium heat, heat olive oil in a large heavy-bottomed soup pan. Brown the chicken on all sides. Remove the chicken, leaving the juices in the pan and maintaining medium heat. Cut the chicken into chunks, and set aside. Add the onions to the pan and cook about 2 minutes or until softened. Sprinkle in cumin and cinnamon, and cook for 1 minute. Carefully stir in the tomatoes, chickpeas, chicken broth, orange juice, cayenne pepper, and the reserved chicken. Reduce heat, cover and simmer for 30 minutes, stirring occasionally. Five minutes before serving, gently stir in the prunes, sweet potatoes, and thawed spinach. Just before serving add the lemon juice, and serve the stew over couscous. Serves 6.

CASABLANCA COUSCOUS

1 box of couscous mix | olive oil

Prepare the couscous according to the package directions for the amount of servings you need.

 Make Ahead of Time

COCONUT ALMOND BRITTLE

1 cup white sugar

1/2 cup corn syrup

1 cup sliced almonds

1 tablespoon butter

1 teaspoon vanilla extract

1 teaspoon baking soda

1 cup flaked coconut

Combine the sugar and corn syrup in a medium, microwave-safe bowl. Microwave on high for 3 minutes. Use potholders to remove the bowl, and stir in the almonds. Caution—the mixture will be very hot! Microwave for 4 more minutes. Carefully stir in the vanilla and butter, and microwave for 1 minute. Add baking soda, and stir until slightly foamy. Pour mixture onto a buttered baking sheet sprinkled with half the coconut. Sprinkle the rest of the coconut on top, and use a buttered spatula to press in the coconut and to thinly spread the mixture on the pan. Let cool until firm. Break into pieces to serve.

 Decorations

Take a trip to Morocco! To help create a Moroccan atmosphere, hang bright, colorful fabrics (or even sheets) around the dining area, draping them loosely over windows and hanging from the ceiling and walls. Use double-stick Velcro, or to attach them carefully without damaging ceilings or walls, hang the fabric over rods propped on supports. If someone in your group has a netted canopy, you can use it to create a special conversation area with lots of cozy pillows to sit on.

For more adventure, try eating Moroccan-style at a low table with pillows on the floor. Decorate tables with colorful candles, brass knickknacks, tiles, mirrors, and mosaics—anything that looks Moroccan.

Burn a stick of incense or a spicy candle to infuse the room with a mysterious aroma.

Station a greeter at the door, and as people arrive have each person pick up a "passport" before entering. To make passports, purchase bright-colored index cards. On each card write the word "Passport." Below it, write the person's name, and on the bottom write Psalm 139:9-10: "If I settle on the far side of the sea, even there your hand will guide me." You can embellish the passports with stick-on jewels, stickers, or drawings. These passports will help remind women that wherever they travel in life, God will always be with them!

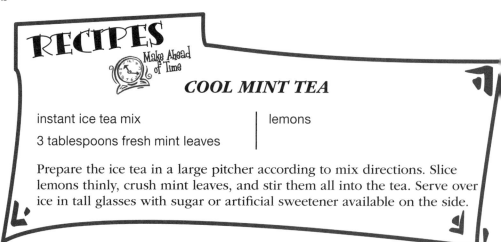

RECIPES
Make Ahead of Time

COOL MINT TEA

instant ice tea mix

3 tablespoons fresh mint leaves

lemons

Prepare the ice tea in a large pitcher according to mix directions. Slice lemons thinly, crush mint leaves, and stir them all into the tea. Serve over ice in tall glasses with sugar or artificial sweetener available on the side.

Mealtime TalkStarters

• Share a story of a travel adventure you've had.

• What do you like or dislike about traveling?

• How do you feel when you are in an unfamiliar place with unfamiliar customs?

• How do you think God helps direct us in our travels through life's unfamiliar challenges and territories?

COOKING TOGETHER

1. Before your group arrives, set out cutting boards, knives, a large heavy-bottomed soup pan, and a smaller saucepan.

2. As people arrive, invite volunteers to help prepare the Moroccan stew according to the recipe on page 61.

3. Ask another volunteer to cut and arrange the watermelon and cantaloupe cubes on plates with toothpicks.

4. After the stew is set to simmer, prepare the couscous according to the package directions for the number of servings you need.

5. Have anyone who isn't busy cooking set the table and prepare a drink for everyone.

6. About five minutes before you serve the meal, practice a traditional Moroccan custom. Fill a large pitcher with lukewarm water, and squeeze a little lemon juice into it. Have the hostess take the pitcher of water and a towel to each person in the group and pour a small amount of water over each woman's fingers. Have another person catch the water in a small basin. Let the women pat their hands dry on the towel. This is also a good time to have someone pray over the meal and your time together.

7. Serve the Moroccan stew over the couscous, and place the plate of fruit on the table.

8. To clean up, put any leftovers in the refrigerator, wash the dishes, or set them aside for later.

9. Encourage women to take pillows with them to the movie room if they would like. Serve the Coconut Almond Brittle and Cool Mint Tea during the movie.

LET'S WATCH A MOVIE!

Casablanca

THE PRE-SHOW

Gather in the area where you will show the movie. Allow time for a quick restroom break.

After everyone has gathered, serve the Coconut Almond Brittle and Cool Mint Tea to those who would like dessert. You can also make the leftover melon available for those who would prefer fruit.

Hand out pens and paper to each person, and have everyone try to answer these trivia questions about the classic movie *Casablanca*. Then see how everyone did!

Casablanca TRIVIA QUIZ

1. What famous line from the movie *Casablanca* is consistently misquoted?

2. Where was Ingrid Bergman born?

3. Name one of Humphrey Bogart's wives.

4. Where was *Casablanca* filmed?

5. How many Academy Awards did *Casablanca* win?

6. Humphrey Bogart improvised what famous line from *Casablanca*?

 Answers

1. "Play it again, Sam." Humphrey Bogart actually said, "You played it for her, you can play it for me. Play it!"

2. Stockholm, Sweden

3. Lauren Bacall, Mayo Methot, Mary Philips, and Helen Menken

4. Entirely in California. Every scene was shot in Burbank, except for the very opening.

5. Three. Best Picture; Best Director; Best Writing, Screenplay

6. "Here's lookin' at you, kid."

THE SHOW
Casablanca

Genre: Drama

Length: 102 minutes

Rating: PG for mild violence, drinking, and adult themes

Plot: Rick Blaine (Humphrey Bogart) is an exiled American who owns a nightclub in Casablanca, a busy connection stop for Europeans fleeing the Germans and seeking refuge in America. Rick comes into possession of two valuable letters of transit and soon discovers his former love, Ilsa (Ingrid Bergman), is in Casablanca and she and her husband, Victor Laszlo, are in need of the letters. Laszlo, a resistance leader wanted by the Germans, needs to get out of the country fast, and Ilsa knows Rick can help. But will he?

Rick and Ilsa, conflicted and torn between feelings for their lost love, duty, honor, and self-sacrifice, finally decide on a plan to escape to America. But which plan will succeed in the end? Will love, duty, or self-sacrifice prevail?

THE POST-SHOW

After the movie, use some or all of these questions to discuss the spiritual themes in *Casablanca*.

What are some of the moral and ethical dilemmas the characters in the movie face? How would you have responded in the same situation?

What do you think caused Rick to tell Ilsa, "I'm the only one I'm interested in now"?

What do you think caused Rick to change his mind and help Ilsa in the end?

Do you think Rick and Ilsa truly loved each other? What about Laszlo and Ilsa? Why or why not?

How do you feel about the way Ilsa handled ending and then rekindling her relationship with Rick? How can you apply this to your own relationships?

How do we respond when others have hurt us or betrayed our trust? How should we respond?

Laszlo said, "Each of us has a destiny for good or for evil." How can we, as Christians, maintain integrity in difficult situations such as the situations the characters in this movie face?

PRAYER

End your night by joining in prayer. Have women pair up to pray. If you have an uneven number of women, make one group of three. Encourage the women to pray for God's direction and protection as they try to live their lives with integrity that is pleasing to him.

Bible Passages
You may want to use these Bible passages during your movie discussion:

- 1 Chronicles 29:17—God is pleased with integrity.

- Proverbs 2:7-8—God guards the course of the just.

- Jeremiah 6:16—Ask God where the good way is, and walk in it.

- Proverbs 10:12—Love covers over all wrongs.

The Princess Bride

Genre: Adventure/Fantasy   **Length:** 98 minutes   **Rating:** PG

QUICK PLOT: *Sword fighting. Torture. Revenge. Giants. Chases. Escapes. True love. Miracles.*

DINNER
Fire-Swamp Fondue
Cheese Fondue
Fezzik's Fruit Platter
Beverages (sparkling cider, coffee)

MOVIE SNACKS
Miracle Max's Chocolate-Covered Pills
Coffee

⌁ SUPPLIES ⌁

Before your Dinner and a Movie event, you may want to talk to everyone in your group and divide the ingredients list. Keep in mind that some items, such as the meats, cost more than others. Perhaps several people would like to share the cost of the meats, while others each bring a couple of items.

What you'll need:	*Names:*

Easy Option Meal

No time to cook? Contact a local restaurant or grocery store for its soup selection. Choose something with a little spice to go with the fire-swamp theme, and ask how much to get for the number of women you are expecting. Pick up bread or rolls and a fruit or vegetable platter to accompany your soup. Choose chocolate-covered cookies, truffles, or dipped chocolates for dessert.

Fire-Swamp Fondue

canola or vegetable oil (about 2 cups per fondue pot) _____

boneless beef sirloin or tenderloin, cut in bite-size pieces (1 to 2 ounces per person) _____

raw chicken breast, cut in bite-size pieces (1 to 2 ounces per person) _____

large raw shrimp, peeled and de-veined (4 to 5 shrimp per person) _____

dipping sauces, such as cocktail sauce, horseradish, mustard, teriyaki, and sweet and sour sauce _____

Cheese Fondue

2 cups medium cheddar cheese, shredded _____

2 tablespoons flour _____

one 10-ounce can condensed cheddar cheese soup _____

3/4 cup milk _____

baguettes, cut into 1-inch squares _____

baby carrots (approximately 5 to 10 carrots per person) _____

cauliflower, cut into bite-size florets (approximately 5 to 10 florets per person) _____

Fezzik's Fruit Platter

fruit, such as apples, pineapple, and seedless grapes _____

lemon juice _____

8-ounce package of cream cheese _____

8-ounce jar of marshmallow creme _____

Extras

sparkling cider _____

coffee _____

Make Ahead of Time

Miracle Max's Chocolate-Covered Pills (recipe on page 68) _____

RECIPES

FIRE-SWAMP FONDUE

cooking oil (canola or vegetable)

boneless beef sirloin or tenderloin, cut in bite-size pieces (1 to 2 ounces per person)

raw chicken breast, cut in bite-size pieces (1 to 2 ounces per person)

large raw shrimp, peeled and deveined (4 to 5 shrimp per person)

dipping sauces, such as cocktail sauce, horseradish, mustard, teriyaki, and sweet and sour sauce

Prepare a large platter for the beef, shrimp, and chicken. Place the meats on the platter in equal thirds, cover with plastic wrap, and keep refrigerated until 5 to 10 minutes before cooking. Put the sauces in different bowls (you can label them if you want) with small serving spoons. Have a metal fondue pot or small cooking pot available for every 4 to 6 people in your group. Fill the pots about half full with the oil, and heat to about 360 degrees. Maintain the heat on the stove or in the pots. Most fondue pots come with a container for an alcohol or "canned heat" product, such as Sterno. This should also include a diffuser so you can adjust the heat intensity by opening or closing the heat source. You will want to make sure the oil is not too hot.

Since fondue is a communal meal, there are some basic rules of etiquette you will want to cover with your guests. First, never put raw meats on the plate you will eat from. Use your fondue fork to spear the meats (you can put up to two pieces on each fork), and put them directly into the oil. Make sure the meats—especially the chicken— are cooked thoroughly before removing. When meats are removed from the pot, use a dining fork to slide the meat off the fondue fork.

CHEESE FONDUE

2 cups medium cheddar cheese, shredded

2 tablespoons flour

one 10-ounce can condensed cheddar cheese soup

3/4 cup milk

baguettes, cut into 1-inch squares

baby carrots (approximately 5 to 10 carrots per person)

cauliflower, cut into bite-size florets (approximately 5 to 10 florets per person)

Heat cheese soup and milk in a slow cooker. Slowly add grated cheddar cheese and flour. Continue to stir until smooth. Consistency should be creamy and smooth. Add milk if needed, and stir well. Serve on medium or low setting. Place bread, carrots, and cauliflower on a platter for dipping. Ingredients for fondue are based on 4 to 6 people. Double or triple if necessary, but use a single pot for each recipe.

Decorations

This is everyone's night to be a princess! Encourage guests to come dressed in princess attire, such as old bridesmaid or prom dresses, and provide toy tiaras for guests to don as they arrive.

This event will take on a medieval theme. Paint bamboo torches black and use them to light the entrance to your house. Use candles and low lighting inside to create a dramatic, medieval feel. Black iron candleholders would be perfect for this occasion.

Serve your fondue out of the fondue pots or cooking pots and place the dipping items on silver platters. You can also cover plates with aluminum foil to create this look. Accent the décor with rosemary sprigs dipped in gold paint. Roll your napkins in silver napkin rings. If you have them, put silver or pewter goblets out on the dinner table next to the sparkling cider.

If you have any classical music, this would be a great time to dust the albums off to set the mood.

RECIPES

FEZZIK'S FRUIT PLATTER

fruit, such as apples, pineapple, and seedless grapes

lemon juice

8-ounce package of cream cheese

8-ounce jar of marshmallow creme

Wash all of the fruit. Slice apples and coat them with a bit of lemon juice to keep them from browning. Chop pineapple into bite-size pieces, and cut grapes into clusters of about 5 to 10 grapes. Arrange the fruit around the edge of a serving platter. In a separate bowl, prepare the fruit dip by mixing cream cheese and marshmallow creme together until smooth. Chill until ready to serve. Place bowl of fruit dip in the center of the platter. The number of women in your group will determine how much fruit you need. Figure about half an apple, 5 chunks of pineapple, and 5 to 10 grapes per woman.

Make Ahead of Time

MIRACLE MAX'S CHOCOLATE-COVERED PILLS

24 ounces semisweet chocolate chips

1 1/4 cups evaporated milk

1/4 cup sugar

2 teaspoons vanilla extract

goodies to dip, such as marshmallows, pound cake, and strawberries

Put the chocolate chips, evaporated milk, sugar, and vanilla extract into a slow cooker. Cover and cook on high for 30 minutes. Stir and cook one more hour on low. If you are transferring the mixture to the Dinner and a Movie event, make sure that it is warm and plug it in immediately when you arrive. The consistency should be creamy and smooth. Add milk if needed, and stir well. Maintain low heat until it's ready to use, stirring occasionally. Cut pound cake into bite-sized pieces, and wash strawberries. Place all dipping goodies on a platter together and serve with chocolate. Makes 8 servings.

COOKING TOGETHER

1. Before the group arrives, prepare the oil in the fondue pots or cooking pots. Keep in mind that you'll need one pot for every 4 to 6 people.

2. When your guests arrive, ask for volunteers to cut the meat and place it on a serving tray. Then they can put the sauces in bowls.

3. Have two other volunteers cut up the bread, vegetables, and fruit. They can prepare the fruit dip according to the recipe on page 68. Cover and refrigerate the dip until you're ready to serve.

4. Assign one person to prepare the Cheese Fondue according to the recipe on page 67.

5. Make sure the chocolate slow cooker is set on low, and stir it occasionally. Add milk if the texture is too thick.

6. Ask anyone who isn't cooking to set the table and prepare beverages for everyone.

7. When everything is ready, set out the meat tray, sauces, vegetables, fruit platter, and fruit dip. Transfer the meat and cheese fondue pots to the table and distribute fondue forks.

8. Have everyone gather around the pots. Ask someone to pray, and then go over fondue etiquette. Then dive in!

9. When you are done, clean up the dishes and put leftovers in the refrigerator.

10. Serve the coffee and Miracle Max's Chocolate-Covered Pills before the movie.

Mealtime TalkStarters

- What was one of your favorite fairy tales when you were younger? Why?

- Describe your perfect prince.

- Tell about something someone did for you that made you feel like a princess.

- Have you ever done something for someone else to make him or her feel like royalty?

- Do you believe in happily-ever-after endings? How about true love? What does the Bible have to say about these two topics?

LET'S WATCH A MOVIE!

The Princess Bride

The Pre-Show

Allow time for a quick restroom break. Serve coffee to anyone who would like some. Set out the chocolate fondue and goodies for dipping. Give everyone a clean plate, napkins, and clean fondue forks. Have the ladies select the items they would like, dip them in chocolate, and put them on their plates. Everyone can take her dessert to the area where you will be showing the movie.

Hand out paper and pens. While the ladies are eating dessert, have them take this Princess Trivia Quiz. Then see how everyone did!

Helpful Hint

For extra fun, have a special tiara or crown—as gaudy as you can get—for the winner of the Princess Trivia Quiz to wear the rest of the night.

Answers

1. Diana, Princess of Wales
2. Princess Leia Organa from *Star Wars*
3. Princess Ariel from Disney's *The Little Mermaid*
4. Grace Kelly, Princess of Monaco
5. Princess Aurora from *Sleeping Beauty*

Princess Trivia Quiz

1. This princess was a kindergarten teacher before finding her prince.

2. This princess is known for the braided buns she wears above her ears.

3. This underwater princess is a bit of a pack rat.

4. This actress turned princess was born in Philadelphia, Pennsylvania.

5. This princess' name is also the name for a luminous atmospheric phenomenon.

The Show
The Princess Bride

Genre: Adventure/Fantasy

Length: 98 minutes

Rating: PG for some violence (swordplay, torture) and language

Plot: A woman named Buttercup (Robin Wright Penn) finds herself in love with Westley (Cary Elwes), a farmhand who leaves to find his fortune across the sea. "I will always come for you," he reassures her. Word gets back to Buttercup that his ship was attacked and her love is dead. She makes a promise to herself that she will "never love again."

Five years later she finds herself engaged to Prince Humperdinck (Chris Sarandon), whose intentions are questionable. A mysterious masked man kidnaps her, and together they must battle swamps, giants, and a Rodent of Unusual Size (R.O.U.S.). With the unlikely help of a revenge-obsessed sword maker, a friendly giant, and a miracle maker, true love and justice eventually prevail in this classic story of adventure.

The Post-Show

After the movie, use some or all of these questions to discuss the spiritual themes of *The Princess Bride.*

What are some of your favorite lines in this movie? How do they relate to your life?

Westley's entire life was devoted to winning back his love. Compare his actions to Christ's actions. How does Westley's love for Buttercup parallel Christ's love for the church?

"As you wish!" was Westley's way of telling Buttercup he loved her. In what small ways does God communicate his love to you every day?

What are some creative ways we can communicate God's love to our friends and family on a daily basis? to those who don't know him?

Westley and Buttercup overcame great obstacles in the fire swamp. Have you had a fire-swamp experience in your life lately? What did you learn during that challenging time?

Westley is a great example of perseverance. What motivated him? How can we apply this to the trials we face in our own lives?

Even when all hope seems lost, Buttercup never gives up hope that she will be saved. What is your response in seemingly desperate situations? Do you have a quiet confidence that God will take care of you?

Bible Passages
You may want to use these Bible passages during your movie discussion:

- Ephesians 5:25—Love as Christ loved.

- Hebrews 12:1—Run your race with perseverance.

- James 1:2-4—Trials develop good character.

PRAYER

End the evening with a prayer together. Ask if there are any specific prayer needs, especially for those who are going through a trial and need God's strength to persevere. Encourage women to think of a way they can learn to show love to others through their actions. Have each woman pray for someone else in the group.

Whale Rider

Genre: Drama **Length:** 101 minutes **Rating:** PG-13

QUICK PLOT: *A young girl struggles to maintain family honor and love while taking the courageous steps necessary to fulfill her destiny.*

DINNER
Maori Tilapia
Kumara Sweet Potato Bake
Kiwi-Strawberry Skewers
Beverages (soda, ice tea, or ice water)

MOVIE SNACKS
Pavlova (national dessert of New Zealand)
Fruit Chillers

❧ SUPPLIES ❧

Before your Dinner and a Movie event, you may want to talk to everyone in the group and divide the ingredients list. Keep in mind that some items, such as tilapia, cost a lot more than others. Perhaps two people would like to share the cost of the tilapia, while others each bring a couple of items.

Easy Option Meal

If you want to embrace a true island attitude for the night and relax instead of cooking, you can find all you need at a grocery store or fast-food restaurant. Purchase fruits such as bananas, grapes, and kiwis for an island fruit bowl. Pick up a quick and easy meal of fish and chips at a local fast-food restaurant or frozen, breaded fish filets and fries at the grocery store. For dessert, you can buy packaged meringues and lemonade.

What you'll need: Names:

Maori Tilapia

one 4-ounce tilapia fillet per person   _____

1/2 cup all-purpose flour   _____

1/2 teaspoon salt   _____

1/4 teaspoon pepper   _____

1/8 teaspoon cayenne pepper   _____

1 to 2 tablespoons butter   _____

1 teaspoon olive oil   _____

1 to 2 lemon slices per person   _____

Make Ahead of Time **Kumara Sweet Potato Bake**   _____
(recipe on page 75)

Kiwi-Strawberry Skewers

3 to 5 fresh strawberries per person   _____

1 medium-sized kiwi per person   _____

one 6-inch wooden skewer per person   _____

Fruit Chillers

5 cups of seedless watermelon, roughly chopped   _____

1/4 cup sugar   _____

juice of 1 lime   _____

Extras

beverages   _____

1 inexpensive shell necklace per person   _____

Make Ahead of Time **Pavlova** (recipe on page 76)   _____

RECIPES

MAORI TILAPIA

one 4-ounce tilapia fillet per
   person (any mild white fish can
   be substituted for tilapia)

1/2 cup all-purpose flour

1/2 teaspoon salt

1/4 teaspoon pepper

1/8 teaspoon cayenne pepper

1 to 2 tablespoons butter

1 teaspoon olive oil

1 to 2 lemon slices per person

Heat a nonstick frying pan over medium-high heat until hot. Add
butter and olive oil. On a plate combine flour, salt, pepper, and
cayenne pepper. Press the tilapia fillets in the mixture, coating both
sides. When butter is melted and sizzling, add tilapia fillets to the
pan. Lightly brown and carefully turn over. Cook until golden. Serve
with lemon slices.

To make this dish a bit lighter, you can broil the fillets. Simply
sprinkle the fillets with salt, pepper, and cayenne, and brush with
a small amount of olive oil. Broil the fish 4 inches from heat for 5
minutes per side or until fish flakes easily with a fork.

Make Ahead of Time

KUMARA SWEET POTATO BAKE

Kumara is the Polynesian name for sweet potato, and it is a staple of
the Maori diet.

4 medium sweet potatoes

1 teaspoon salt

1 tablespoon corn starch

1/2 cup packed brown sugar

1 cup orange juice

1/4 cup seedless raisins

2 tablespoons chopped walnuts

1/2 teaspoon grated orange rind

orange slices (for garnish)

Preheat oven to 400 degrees. Wash sweet potatoes and place on a
baking sheet. Bake for 1 hour. Let the sweet potatoes cool until they
can be handled. Preheat oven to 350 degrees. Peel sweet potatoes and
slice in half lengthwise. Arrange potatoes in a shallow baking pan.
Sprinkle with 3/4 teaspoon salt. Combine corn starch, brown sugar,
and remaining 1/4 teaspoon salt in a separate small saucepan. Stir in
orange juice and raisins. Bring to a boil while stirring. Add remaining
ingredients, and pour the mixture over the potatoes. Bake uncovered
for 20 minutes. Garnish with orange slices. Serves about 6 people.

Decorations

To get guests in the island mood,
decorate with a Polynesian theme.
Decorate the dining room with palm
branches or other greenery. Set
seashells on the dining table and around
the room.

Use a large glass bowl filled with water
and floating candles or flower petals as
a centerpiece. To mimic a beach setting,
you could also cover the table with a
plastic tablecloth, and make sand piles
on it. Or pour sand into glass bowls,
and set small seashells and beautiful
stones or marbles in the sand. Use
small umbrellas to embellish beverage
glasses, and look for island-themed
napkins and paper plates.

Encourage women to come decked
out in their finest island gear, such as
sarongs and sandals. Hawaiian shirts
will work, too! You could even purchase
grass skirts for women to wear over
their clothing.

Before guests arrive, spray floral-
scented room sprays or light floral-
scented candles to further enhance
the atmosphere. During the meal
preparation and dinner, play a CD of
ocean sounds such as waves crashing
or whales singing.

RECIPES

KIWI-STRAWBERRY SKEWERS

3 to 5 fresh strawberries per person

1 medium-sized kiwi per person

one 6-inch wooden skewer per person

Wash fruit, and peel kiwis. Cut strawberries and kiwis into quarters. Slide fruit pieces onto skewers, alternating kiwi and strawberry for presentation.

 Make Ahead of Time

PAVLOVA (NATIONAL DESSERT OF NEW ZEALAND)

2 egg whites

8 tablespoons superfine sugar

1 teaspoon vanilla extract

Preheat oven to 250 degrees. Line a cookie sheet with parchment paper. Beat the egg whites until stiff but not dry. (When the beaters are lifted, the eggs should form peaks that stand straight up.) Add 6 tablespoons of the sugar, 1 spoonful at a time, while beating well after each addition. Add the vanilla extract and fold in the remaining sugar.

Use a pastry bag with a tube or a spoon to shape the meringues into small dollops on the cookie sheet. Bake for 1 hour. *Turn off the oven without opening the door.* Let the meringues remain in the oven for another 6 hours to dry out so they're crisp. Makes 24 to 36 meringues.

FRUIT CHILLERS

5 cups seedless watermelon, roughly chopped

1/4 cup sugar

juice of 1 lime

Combine watermelon, sugar, and lime juice in blender. Blend until liquid. Pour through a strainer into a large pitcher. Skim foam from the juice, and serve! Serves approximately 4.

COOKING TOGETHER

1. Prepare the Pavlova ahead of time, keeping in mind the meringues need to sit in the oven for six hours. Before the guests arrive, prepare the Kumara Sweet Potato Bake. You'll want to put the Sweet Potato Bake in the oven around the time guests arrive.

2. As each woman arrives, "lei" her with a shell necklace (found at most party stores). When everyone has arrived, invite two volunteers to prepare the Kiwi-Strawberry Skewers according to the recipe on page 76.

3. Have another two volunteers coat the tilapia fillets and begin browning them in the frying pan.

4. Ask one or two other women to prepare the Fruit Chillers according to the recipe on page 76, and then put it in the fridge to cool for later.

5. When the Kumara Sweet Potato Bake has finished baking, have someone take it from the oven and garnish it with orange slices.

6. Encourage those who aren't busy cooking to set the table and prepare drinks for everyone.

7. When the tilapia fillets are golden, take them out of the pan and serve with lemon slices. Have each woman prepare a plate; then gather at the table. Ask someone to pray over the meal, and then enjoy!

8. When you've finished eating, work together to clear the table and clean the dishes (or you may set the dishes aside and wash them later). Put any leftovers in the refrigerator.

9. Serve the Pavlova and Fruit Chillers during the movie.

Mealtime TalkStarters

- What's your favorite memory of the ocean (or any other body of water if you've never visited the ocean)?

- The Kumara Sweet Potato Bake is a traditional New Zealand dish. What is a traditional dish in your family or culture?

- Why are traditions and rituals so important? When, if ever, is it OK for a tradition to be broken?

- Tell a favorite story about your father or grandfather.

- Tell about a dream or goal you've had since you were very young. If there is one thing you think you were born to be or do, what is it?

LET'S WATCH A MOVIE!

Whale Rider

THE PRE-SHOW

Have everyone gather in the area where you'll show the movie. If you have just finished eating dinner together, you may want to provide a quick restroom break.

When everyone has gathered, serve the Pavlova and Fruit Chillers to anyone who wants dessert. Be sure to provide napkins. Hand out paper and pens, and have everyone answer these fun trivia questions about New Zealand.

Read the answers and see how everyone did. Invite everyone to tell about her favorite movie set in another country or culture.

Answers

1. *Kiwis*

2. a. *Aotearoa* means "Land of the Long White Cloud."

3. Rugby football

4. The Maori. The Maori are the indigenous people of New Zealand, coming from their Polynesian homeland of Hawaiki.

5. The bungee jump, the tranquillizer gun, and electric fences are all New Zealand inventions.

6. In 1893, New Zealand was the first country to give women full rights to vote. However, women were not given the right to be elected until later.

7. c. New Zealand is 268,680 square kilometers, including several sets of islands. That's almost 104,000 square miles, very close to the size of Colorado.

NEW ZEALAND TRIVIA QUIZ

1. What is the informal term for native New Zealanders?

2. What is the meaning of the native name for New Zealand, *Aotearoa*?

    a. Land of the Long White Cloud

    b. Land of the Blue-Green Sea

    c. Land of the Big Blue Sky

3. What is the most popular spectator sport in New Zealand?

4. Who were the first people to migrate to New Zealand?

5. Name one thing that was invented in New Zealand.

6. New Zealand was the first country to give women the right to do what?

7. What U.S. state is approximately the size of New Zealand?

    a. Massachusetts

    b. California

    c. Colorado

THE SHOW
Whale Rider

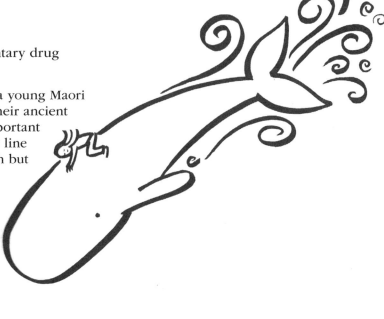

Genre: Drama

Length: 101 minutes

Rating: Rated PG-13 for brief language and a momentary drug reference.

Plot: Keisha Castle-Hughes plays Paikea Whangara, a young Maori girl in modern-day New Zealand. Her people hold their ancient tribal traditions in high esteem. One of the most important traditions is the bloodline of the chief. Pai broke the line of firstborn sons when her twin brother died in birth but she lived.

Pai's grandfather, Koro, whose hopes of his own family carrying on the line have been crushed, must now choose a new chief. Koro refuses to acknowledge that a girl could fill the role of chief, but Pai knows she has a distinct role to play in the salvation of her people, and she has talents and visions that reveal she is meant to lead her people.

THE POST-SHOW

After the movie, use some or all of these questions to discuss the spiritual themes in *Whale Rider*.

Pai's people have reverence for their cultural heritage and the ancestors who came before. As Christians, what is our heritage? What does the Bible say about our "ancestors"—the forefathers of our faith?

Pai knew she had a unique purpose. As Christians, what is our unique purpose and calling? How can you fulfill that purpose in everyday life?

Pai had to overcome the barriers of cultural tradition and even her own grandfather in pursuing her destiny. When have you pursued something you felt you had to do and encountered barriers? What happened?

Describe the balance between respecting authority, such as your parents or the law, while also obeying God and doing what you know is right.

What potential do you think God sees in you? How can you claim your true identity in God and live out this potential?

What role did courage play in this movie? What do you need courage for in your life right now?

Discuss how Pai's actions are similar to those of Jesus Christ.

How did people resist Jesus as the Chosen One? How do people resist his true identity now? What is *your* personal response to Jesus?

Bible Passages
You may want to use these Bible passages during your movie discussion:

- Psalm 138:8—God made each of us for a purpose.

- 1 Peter 2:9-10—We are a chosen people.

- Ephesians 6:1-3—Honor and respect your parents.

- Joshua 1:6-9—Be strong and courageous.

Prayer

End the evening by praying together. Encourage each person to share one specific way to put into practice the lessons learned from the movie *Whale Rider*. Have each woman pray for someone else in the group. Tell women that the shell leis are theirs to keep. Each time they see or wear their leis, they can be reminded of the lessons learned from *Whale Rider*.

Enchanted April

Genre: Drama   **Length:** 95 minutes   **Rating:** PG

QUICK PLOT: *Four women rent a castle in Italy to escape their dreary lives in rainy, post–World War I London. There they rediscover the beauty and sunshine of life and experience an opening of their once shuttered hearts.*

DINNER
Pasta With Fresh Tomato Sauce
Walnut Salad
Focaccia Bread
Beverages (ice water, coffee, hot tea)

MOVIE SNACKS
Assorted Biscotti and Cookies
Coffee
Hot Tea and Fresh Lemons

SUPPLIES

Before your Dinner and a Movie event, you may want to talk to the women in your small group and divide the ingredients list. For this Italian meal, try to get the freshest ingredients possible. Fresh pasta is preferable over dry processed varieties and is available in the refrigerated section of your local grocery store. Fresh tomato sauce and grated Parmesan cheese are also available in this section. Two women could share the cost of these more expensive ingredients, while others could bring one or two of the other items.

What you'll need: Names:

Pasta With Fresh Tomato Sauce
2 packages fresh pasta (spaghetti or fettuccini)   _____

4 cups canned Italian plum tomatoes, or 4 pounds fresh ripe Roma tomatoes   _____

1 stick (8 tablespoons) butter   _____

1 large onion, peeled and cut in half   _____

salt   _____

fresh chopped basil   _____

freshly grated Parmesan cheese   _____

Walnut Salad
1 head Romaine lettuce   _____

1/4 pound imported Gorgonzola cheese   _____

1/2 cup shelled walnuts, chopped   _____

1/4 cup red wine vinegar (or to taste)   _____

1/4 cup olive oil (or to taste)   _____

salt   _____

pepper   _____

Extras
focaccia bread   _____

biscotti (assorted varieties)   _____

assorted Italian-style cookies (Milano, almond, or lemon cookies)   _____

beverages   _____

Easy Option Meal

If you would like an easier option, boil a pot of spaghetti, and serve with your favorite brand of spaghetti sauce. Use packaged salad mix and fresh focaccia or garlic bread from the grocery store. For dessert, buy some biscotti or your favorite Milano cookies and serve with coffee and tea.

RECIPES

PASTA WITH FRESH TOMATO SAUCE

2 packages fresh pasta (spaghetti or fettuccini)

4 cups canned Italian plum tomatoes, or 4 pounds fresh ripe Roma tomatoes

1 stick (8 tablespoons) butter

1 large onion, peeled and cut in half

salt

fresh chopped basil

freshly grated Parmesan cheese

Plunge the tomatoes into boiling water for a little less than a minute. Drain, and when cool enough to handle, skin them and cut them into small pieces or purée in food processor. Place the tomatoes in a large saucepan. Add the butter, onion, and salt to taste. Cook uncovered at a slow simmer for 45 minutes. Stir occasionally and mash any large pieces of tomato. Discard the onion before serving. (If you prefer a meat sauce, add 1/2 to 1 pound cooked ground beef or Italian sausage.)

Serve over fresh pasta cooked according to package directions. Top with freshly grated Parmesan cheese and fresh chopped basil. Serves 6 to 8.

WALNUT SALAD

1 head Romaine lettuce

1/4 pound imported Gorgonzola cheese

1/2 cup shelled walnuts, chopped

1/4 cup red wine vinegar (or to taste)

1/4 cup olive oil (or to taste)

salt

pepper

Wash and tear the lettuce into bite-size pieces and place in a large salad bowl. In a small serving bowl, mix the olive oil, vinegar, a pinch of salt, and pepper. Beat the ingredients with a fork until evenly blended.

Mash half the Gorgonzola cheese with a fork and add it, along with half the walnuts, to the dressing. Pour over the lettuce and toss to coat. Top with the remaining Gorgonzola and walnuts, and serve immediately. Serves approximately 6.

Helpful Hint

To make this dinner a bit lighter, decrease the amount of olive oil in the dressing to taste, or serve the dressing on the side. You can also reduce the amount of butter used in the tomato sauce to taste.

Decorations

Escape the everyday trappings of life, and travel with your friends to an enchanted Italian villa. For a nice centerpiece, buy bunches of grapes and arrange them in a silver bowl. Set out goblets to use for your beverages, and dig out those little-used linen tablecloths and napkins. To give the table an eclectic, charming look, ask each woman to bring her favorite place setting to use (china or otherwise). Encourage your group to dress in comfortable, flowing clothes that make them feel beautiful.

To help create the mood of an idyllic villa retreat, borrow travel books from the library with pictures of Italian scenery and castles to set on coffee tables. Play any Italian music you own softly in the background, or borrow Italian CDs, such as *The Best of the Three Tenors*, or Andrea Bocelli's *A Night in Tuscany,* from the library.

To make your Italian villa experience even more realistic, enlist a few teens to assist as "servants" for the night to serve and clean up after dinner. This will allow women freedom to enjoy the time without responsibilities.

COOKING TOGETHER

Mealtime TalkStarters

- Share the story of your place setting—its history and why you like it.

- Tell about the last time you ate a meal with china, crystal, and tablecloths at home. Discuss why you think we do it so infrequently.

- Share about places to which you enjoy traveling or would like to travel, and your favorite getaway spot.

- Tell about your favorite place to visit as a child and what made it special to you.

1. Before your group arrives, peel, chop, and begin cooking the tomatoes. Set out a salad bowl and a large saucepan to cook the pasta. (The tomato sauce will need to simmer for 45 minutes before serving.)

2. As people arrive, have women put their place settings on the dining table.

3. Invite volunteers to help prepare the pasta and salad according to the recipes on page 83.

4. Have one person cut the bread and place it on the table with a butter dish.

5. Ask volunteers to set the table and place the salad, freshly grated Parmesan cheese, and the fresh basil on the table just before the meal. They can also prepare drinks for everyone.

6. When the pasta is ready, serve each woman pasta and sauce.

7. Invite someone to pray over the meal, and make a toast to your time together at your enchanted Italian escape!

8. Work together to clean up (unless you have servants!) and wash the china and crystal. Put any leftovers in the refrigerator, and blow out the candles.

9. Refill drinks and serve coffee and hot tea with lemon. Set out a tray of biscotti and cookies to enjoy during the movie.

LET'S WATCH A MOVIE!

Enchanted April

THE PRE-SHOW

Gather in the area where you will show the movie. Allow time for a quick restroom break.

After everyone has gathered, offer hot tea and coffee and set out the cookie tray for those who would like dessert. Give women each a pen and paper and ask them to write their answers to the What Makes Me Happy Quiz.

WHAT MAKES ME HAPPY QUIZ

1. What color makes you feel joyful?

2. What is the most beautiful place you have ever seen or experienced?

3. Where is your favorite place to eat dinner?

4. What makes you laugh?

5. What would your perfect day look like?

6. What is your favorite flower?

 Answers

Encourage your group to briefly share their answers with one another and take a few minutes to explore the similarities and differences in their responses. There are no right or wrong answers. After the movie your group will discuss their answers again during follow-up discussion.

The Show
Enchanted April

Genre: Drama

Length: 95 minutes

Rating: PG for mature themes (implied adultery)

Plot: Lottie (Josie Lawrence) and Rose (Miranda Richardson) are two proper Englishwomen captivated by an advertisement for the vacation of a lifetime: a month's stay in a medieval castle on the Italian Riviera. Desperate to escape their dreary and passionless lives in post–World War I England, they enlist two other women, a beautiful socialite (Polly Walker) and an elderly dowager (Joan Plowright), to share the expense and set off for an idyllic getaway.

Their time at the castle transforms them, and they discover the fulfilling relationships, hope, and love that have long eluded them. Their hearts are reawakened to lost beauty, and the joy in their lives is restored.

The Post-Show

After the movie, use some or all of these questions to discuss the spiritual themes in *Enchanted April.*

? How were each of the women in this movie (Lottie, Rose, Caroline, and Mrs. Fisher) transformed while at the castle?

? Why do you think the location had such an influence on the restoration of their relationships?

? How does location affect your attitudes and relationships? Since we can't always be at an Italian villa, how can we find beauty and joy in our everyday lives?

? The Bible says, "God is love." What do you think Lottie meant when she said the castle was "a tub of love"?

? What did the women each find at the villa that they had lost (or never had)?

? Which character do you think had the most influence on the others? Why?

? Take out your "What Makes Me Happy" list, and discuss how you feel about your answers after watching the movie. What truly makes you happy and joyful in life?

? Share with each other how the message of this movie impacted you personally and how you can practically apply what you learned to your life.

Bible Passages
You may want to use these Bible passages during your movie discussion:

- 1 John 4:16—God is love.

- Isaiah 61:3—God gives beauty and joy.

- Ecclesiastes 3:11-13—God's gift is satisfaction in hard work.

- 1 Corinthians 13:8—Love never fails.

Prayer

End your night by joining in prayer. Have women pair up to share their prayer requests and pray for one another. Then gather the women together and pray over the entire group for continued fullness of beauty, joy, and love in their lives.

Bend It Like Beckham

Genre: Comedy/Drama **Length:** 112 minutes **Rating:** PG-13

QUICK PLOT: *Two teenagers from completely different backgrounds deal with personal challenges and their families' expectations as they pursue their soccer-playing dreams.*

DINNER
Aloo Gobi
Italian Bread
Beverages (soda, ice tea, or ice water)

MOVIE SNACKS
Soccer Ball Sugar Cookies
Mango Milkshakes

❧ SUPPLIES ❧

Before your Dinner and a Movie event, you may want to talk to everyone in the group and divide the ingredients list. Keep in mind that some items, such as Aloo Gobi, cost a lot more than others. Perhaps several people would like to share the cost of the Aloo Gobi, while others each bring a couple of items.

What you'll need: **Names:**

Aloo Gobi

1/2 cup vegetable oil
_____

1 large onion per 3 people
_____

1 large bunch of fresh coriander
_____

1 to 3 small green chilies
_____

1 large cauliflower per 3 people
_____

1 tin whole, peeled tomatoes
_____

1 large potato per person
_____

fresh ginger
_____

fresh garlic, chopped
_____

1 tablespoon cumin seeds
_____

2 teaspoons turmeric
_____

2 teaspoons salt
_____

2 teaspoons garam masala (a spice blend found in the international aisle of most grocery stores)
_____

Extras

butter or margarine
_____

1 loaf Italian bread per 6 people
_____

beverages
_____

Make Ahead of Time **Soccer Ball Sugar Cookies** (recipe on page 90)

Mango Milkshakes (recipe on page 90)
_____

Easy Option Meal

If you want an easy Indian-themed meal, pick up a pre-made chicken curry dish from a local restaurant or grocery-store deli, and serve it with a couple of fresh mangoes. Or for a British theme, make bangers and mash by serving brats with instant mashed potatoes. Pick up sports drinks at the grocery store to go with the sports theme.

RECITES

ALOO GOBI

"Who wants to cook Aloo Gobi when you can bend a ball like Beckham?" You do!

1/2 cup vegetable oil	fresh ginger
1 large onion per 3 people	fresh garlic, chopped
1 large bunch of fresh coriander	1 tablespoon cumin seeds
1 to 3 small green chilies	2 teaspoons turmeric
1 large cauliflower per 3 people	2 teaspoons salt
1 tin whole, peeled tomatoes	2 teaspoons garam masala
1 large potato per person	

Peel and cut the onion into small pieces. Separate leaves from cauliflower and cut cauliflower into eight equal pieces. Divide the fresh coriander into stalks and leaves, and chop coriander. Chop chilies. Peel potatoes and chop into equal pieces. Grate tomatoes, and peel and grate ginger. Mince garlic.

In a large saucepan, heat vegetable oil. Combine onion and cumin seeds in oil. Stir mixture together over heat. When onions are translucent and golden in color, add coriander stalks, salt, and turmeric. Add chilies (1 for mild, 2 for medium, and 3 for spicy-hot). Add tomatoes and stir entire mixture together. Add ginger and garlic, and stir thoroughly until well-mixed.

Add the potatoes and cauliflower to the mixture. Also, to guarantee that nothing sticks to the bottom of the saucepan, include 3 to 4 tablespoons of water. Completely coat potatoes and cauliflower with sauce.

Cover saucepan. Let simmer for 20 minutes (watching for potatoes to be done). Stir in garam masala, and sprinkle coriander leaves over the top of the dish. Turn off the heat and keep the Aloo Gobi covered. Serves 4.

Helpful Hint

This traditional Indian recipe can certainly seem daunting at first, so here are a few tips (just don't let any Indian grandmothers know that you used them!):
- *Watch the "Who Wants to Cook Aloo Gobi" feature on the Bend It Like Beckham DVD while cooking with your girlfriends. You'll get some helpful tips, and you'll feel like you're on a cooking show!*
- *This may be cooking sacrilege, but to keep costs and time spent chopping down, substitute ground spices for fresh. Use 1 teaspoon chili powder instead of fresh chilies, 1/4 teaspoon ground ginger, and 1 teaspoon of ground cumin.*
- *If it's just the name that's throwing you off, it's simple. Aloo means potato, and Gobi means cauliflower.*

Decorations

Decorate for this event by blending a soccer theme and an Indian theme to set the perfect mood for this movie.

Gather soccer posters and put them up on the walls around the dining room. (If you don't have any posters, you can easily make some with poster board and markers. Draw pictures of soccer balls, jerseys with the number 7 for David Beckham, or mascots of local soccer teams embellished with the team name.) You can also hang multicolored sports flags and banners. Gather as many soccer balls as you can and place them in the corners. If you don't have any soccer balls, ask women in the group to bring any they might have.

You might also get some material or mesh that resembles a goal net and drape it in the corners of the movie-watching room. Use masking or electrical tape to draw the markings of a soccer field on the floor.

Hang colorful fabric from the light fixtures and chairs in the dining-room table. Purchase inexpensive, multicolored scarves for everyone to wear. Encourage everyone to come in any sports-themed or Indian clothes they have.

Look for soccer-themed napkins and glasses. Play Indian music in the background during the meal preparation and dinner. You can play the music video on the *Bend It Like Beckham* DVD, use the movie soundtrack, or download popular Indian music from the Internet.

RECIPES

 **Make Ahead of Time**

SOCCER BALL SUGAR COOKIES

1 roll sugar cookie dough

1 container white frosting

black food coloring (or chocolate frosting)

Slice and bake cookies per directions on dough wrapper. When cool, frost cookies with black and white frosting in the design of a soccer ball.

MANGO MILKSHAKES

4 scoops vanilla ice cream per person

1/2 cup mango pulp per person (1 medium-sized mango per 3 to 4 people)

Peel the skin off of the mangoes with a potato peeler. Slice the fruit off of the flat seed in the center of the mango. Combine ice cream and mango pulp in a blender. Blend until smooth. Refrigerate until ready to drink; then pour into glasses and serve.

COOKING TOGETHER

1. Before the group arrives, peel and chop the ingredients for the Aloo Gobi, and prepare the sauce (follow the first two paragraphs of the recipe).

2. When everyone arrives, invite volunteers to add the potatoes and cauliflower and finish preparing the Aloo Gobi according to the recipe on page 89. Keep the dish covered until you're ready to eat.

3. Have someone slice the bread and spread butter or margarine on each slice. Wrap the loaf in foil and put it in a 350-degree oven until the bread is hot and the butter is melted—about 10 to 15 minutes.

4. Ask those who aren't busy cooking to set the table and prepare drinks for everyone.

5. Uncover the Aloo Gobi, and set the dish on the table. Take the bread out of the oven, and place it on the table using the foil as a basket.

6. Invite everyone to gather at the table. Ask someone to pray over the meal, and enjoy!

7. Work together to clear the table and clean the dishes (or set the dishes aside and wash them later). Put any leftovers in the refrigerator.

8. Prepare the Mango Milkshakes, and serve them with the Soccer Ball Sugar Cookies during the movie. See recipes on page 90.

Mealtime TalkStarters

• Tell your favorite sports memory—either as a spectator or participant.

• The girls in this movie plastered the walls of their rooms with pictures of their soccer hero, David Beckham. What did you hang on the walls of your room when you were younger?

• Tell about a close friendship you've had with someone from a completely different background, culture, or race.

• In Indian culture, there is an expectation that girls will learn how to cook traditional foods, such as Aloo Gobi. What are expectations you grew up with? How have you lived up to them or not?

LET'S WATCH A MOVIE!

Bend It Like Beckham

The Pre-Show

Ask everyone to gather in the area where you'll show the movie. If you have just finished eating dinner together, you may want to provide a quick restroom break. When everyone has gathered, serve Soccer Ball Sugar Cookies and Mango Milkshakes to anyone who wants dessert.

Hand out paper and pens, and have everyone answer these fun trivia questions about great women athletes. Then see how everyone did! Invite women to discuss their favorite women athletes.

Women Athletes Trivia Quiz

1. How many Olympic medals has track star Jackie Joyner-Kersee won overall?

2. What speed skater won a record five gold medals over three Olympic Games?

3. In addition to her world record–setting sprinting, what was Florence Griffith Joyner known for?

4. What soccer player has led her team to two World Cup championships?

5. What champion figure skater made famous the "wedge" hairstyle in the 1970s and 1980s?

6. In what year did teams from England and France play each other in the first women's international soccer match?

     a. 1920

     b. 1940

     c. 1960

 Answers

1. Three gold, one silver, and two bronze medals (in the 1984, 1988, 1992, and 1996 Olympic Games)
2. Bonnie Blair
3. Her fashionable appearance—stylish unitards and glamorous fingernails
4. Mia Hamm
5. Dorothy Hamill
6. a. 1920 (although this sport is called football—not soccer—outside of America!)

THE SHOW
Bend It Like Beckham

Genre: Comedy/Drama

Length: 112 minutes

Rating: PG-13 for language and sexual content (crude references in conversation, engaged couple makes out in a car)

Plot: In and near modern-day London, 18-year-olds Jesminder "Jess" Bhamra (Parminder Nagra) and Juliette "Jules" Paxton (Keira Knightley) idolize their hero David Beckham and dream about becoming professional soccer players.

Jess belongs to a traditional Indian family who tolerated her soccer playing when she was younger but now wants her to focus on finding a nice Indian boyfriend, learning to cook traditional Indian dishes, and going to "uni" (university). Jules is on a women's soccer team, but she also faces pressure from home. Her father encourages her talent, but her mother despairs of Jules' athletic pursuits, the way she dresses, and her lack of a boyfriend.

Jules and Jess meet and bond over soccer; Jess tries out for Jules' team and wins a spot. However, when Jess tells her parents the good news, they forbid her from playing because they fear that she'll be badly influenced by the "English girls." They're afraid they'll be shamed as a family and are worried about what their upper-class acquaintances will think. Jess and Jules wrestle with identity issues, relationship conflict, racial prejudice, and their families' expectations. Both must make tough choices between making their families happy and following their own dreams.

THE POST-SHOW

Bible Passages

You may want to use these Bible passages during your movie discussion:

- Psalm 34:12-13—Do not lie.
- 1 Timothy 4:7-8—Train physically *and* spiritually.
- Philippians 3:10-14—Strive toward the eternal prize.

After the movie, use some or all of these questions to discuss the spiritual themes in *Bend It Like Beckham*.

Which character did you relate to the most in this movie? Why?

Were Jess' parents' expectations and actions justified? When have you felt pressure from your parents or another authority figure to be someone you're not or do something you didn't want to do? How did you react?

If you are a parent or caregiver, describe the necessary balance between allowing a child to pursue a dream and the responsibilities or expectations you feel are necessary for their lives.

Jess went behind her parents' backs and lied to them. As Christians, what is the balance between honoring authority or personal responsibility and pursuing a dream?

The women in this movie train hard physically to become great soccer players. What is the value of *spiritual* training? How might we train hard in our Christian faith?

How did Jesus encourage breaking tradition? How did he empower women to choose different social roles?

What is something you're striving for with all your heart and strength? Is it a dream worth striving for? If so, from what friends will you ask for help? How will you ask God for help?

What does God tell us about uncertainty? the unknown? What uncertainties can you put confidently in God's care?

PRAYER

End the evening by praying together. Ask for prayer requests. Encourage each person to share one specific way to put into practice the lessons learned from the movie *Bend It Like Beckham*. Have each person pray for someone else in the group.

THEME INDEX